# Vocabulary
## in Context

**FOR THE COMMON CORE STANDARDS**

## Grade
# 2

# Table of Contents








Vocabulary in Context G2, SV 9780547625751

Vocabulary in Context G2, SV 9780547625751

# Introduction

Steck-Vaughn's *Vocabulary in Context* series offers parents and educators high-quality, curriculum-based products that align with the Common Core Standards for English Language Arts for grades 2–9.

Each unit in the *Vocabulary in Context* books includes:

- fiction and/or nonfiction selections, covering a wide variety of topics
- context activities, ascertaining that children understand what they have read
- vocabulary activities, challenging children to show their understanding of key vocabulary
- questions in a standardized-test format, helping prepare children for standardized exams
- word skills activities, targeting additional vocabulary words and vocabulary skills
- writing activities, providing assignments that encourage children to use the vocabulary words

Reading

**A Special Forest**

**Read the passage below. Think about the meanings of the words in dark print.**

You are in a forest. It is so dark you can barely see the tree trunks around you. Few plants grow in the ground, so it is easy to walk around. You can hear monkeys high above you. You're in a **rain forest**!

A rain forest can be found somewhere that is warm and wet all year. The trees in the rain forest are always green. Some have beautiful flowers. **Fruit** grows on other trees. The fruit is food for the many animals in the rain forest. Some animals in the rain forest live their whole lives in the tops of the trees.

The trees in the rain forest are different **sizes**. Some are very tall, while others are shorter. Because of this, rain forests have several **levels**. The taller trees **form** the forest roof. The tops of shorter trees make a lower level. All the levels of tree **branches** keep light from getting to the forest floor.

Today the rain forests are in **danger**. People cut down the trees. **Pollution** kills the trees. If we don't work hard to save the rain forests, they might be lost forever.

**Go back to the passage. Underline the words or sentences that give you a clue to the meaning of each word in dark print.**

www.harcourtschoolsupply.com
© HMH Supplemental Publishers Inc. All rights reserved. 8 Unit 1
Vocabulary in Context G2, SV 9780547625751

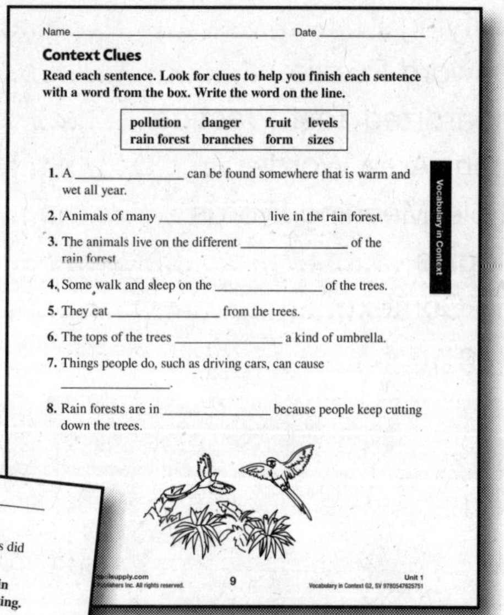

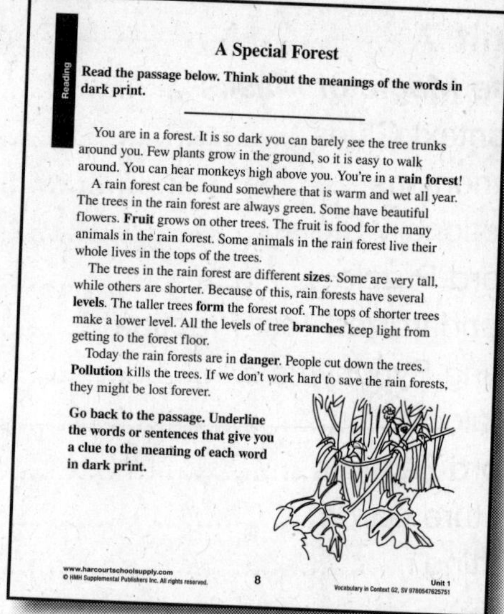

**Reading selection**

Name ______ Date ______

**Context Clues**

**Read each sentence. Look for clues to help you finish each sentence with a word from the box. Write the word on the line.**

| | | | |
|---|---|---|---|
| pollution | danger | fruit | levels |
| rain forest | branches | form | sizes |

1. A ______ can be found somewhere that is warm and wet all year.
2. Animals of many ______ live in the rain forest.
3. The animals live on the different ______ of the rain forest.
4. Some walk and sleep on the ______ of the trees.
5. They eat ______ from the trees.
6. The tops of the trees ______ a kind of umbrella.
7. Things people do, such as driving cars, can cause ______.
8. Rain forests are in ______ because people keep cutting down the trees.

Vocabulary in Context

...schoolsupply.com
...Publishers Inc. All rights reserved. 9 Unit 1
Vocabulary in Context G2, SV 9780547625751

**Vocabulary in Context activity**

Name ______ Date ______

**Onomatopoeia**

There are many words that describe sounds.

bellow croak hoot warble yowl

**Read the sound words in the box above. Write the words in the categories below. Add other words to complete each category.**

| LOUD SOUNDS | QUIET SOUNDS | GRUFF SOUNDS |
|---|---|---|
| 1. bang | 3. hush | 5. grunt |
| **ANIMAL SOUNDS** | **WEATHER SOUNDS** | **MUSIC SOUNDS** |
| 2. yowl | 4. whoosh | 6. toot-toot |

Word Skills

www.harcourtschoolsupply.com
© HMH Supplemental Publishers Inc. All rights reserved. 13 Unit 1
Vocabulary in Context G2, SV 9780547625751

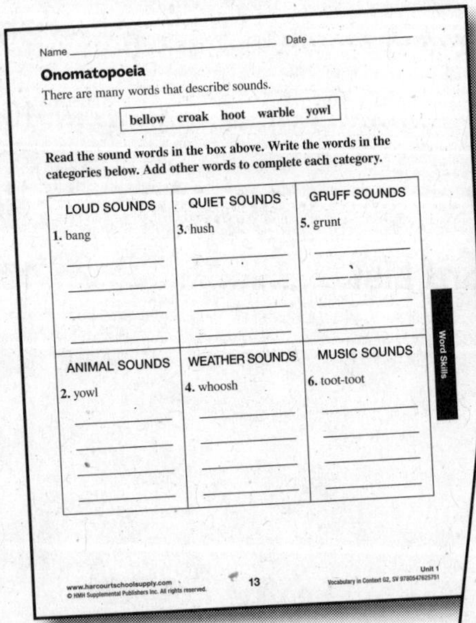

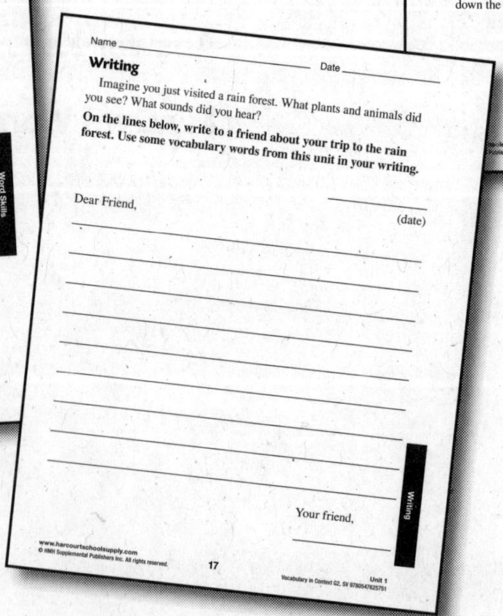

**Word Skills activity**

Name ______ Date ______

**Writing**

Imagine you just visited a rain forest. What plants and animals did you see? What sounds did you hear?

**On the lines below, write to a friend about your trip to the rain forest. Use some vocabulary words from this unit in your writing.**

(date)

Dear Friend,

Your friend,

Writing

www.harcourtschoolsupply.com
© HMH Supplemental Publishers Inc. All rights reserved. 17 Unit 1
Vocabulary in Context G2, SV 9780547625751

**Writing activity**

## Homophones

Homophones are words that sound the same but have different meanings and usually have different spellings.

| | | |
|---|---|---|
| ant—aunt | groan—grown | right—write |
| ate—eight | heal—heel | road—rode—rowed |
| base—bass | here—hear | sail—sale |
| be—bee | hi—high | sea—see |
| beach—beech | hoarse—horse | seen—scene |
| bear—bare | hole—whole | sew—sow—so |
| beat—beet | hour—our | sight—cite—site |
| berry—bury | I—eye | some—sum |
| blew—blue | made—maid | son—sun |
| bored—board | meat—meet | sore—soar |
| bow—bough | new—knew | stair—stare |
| brake—break | no—know | steal—steel |
| buy—by | oar—or | their—there—they're |
| cell—sell | one—won | through—threw |
| cent—sent—scent | pail—pale | to—too—two |
| close—clothes | pain—pane | wail—whale |
| dear—deer | pair—pear | wait—weight |
| flew—flu | peace—piece | way—weigh |
| flour—flower | peek—peak | weak—week |
| for—four | plane—plain | we'll—wheel |
| forth—fourth | principal—principle | wood—would |

# Homographs

Homographs are words that are spelled the same but have different meanings and different origins (*bat*—the mammal, *bat*—the club). Some homographs also have different pronunciations (*august*— majestic, *August*—eighth month).

close < shut / near

dove < pigeon / did dive

live < to exist / having life

desert < abandon / arid land

object < thing / disagree

record < to make note of / best achievement

tear < rip / drop of water from an eye

refuse < to say no / trash

lead < heavy metal / to be first

does < form of *do* / female deer

# Prefixes

Prefixes are letter groups added before a base word to change or add to the word's meaning.

| Prefix | Meaning | Example |
| --- | --- | --- |
| *auto-* | self | autobiography |
| *bi-* | two | bicycle, biweekly |
| *dis-* | not | disbelief |
| *im-* | not | impossible |
| *in-* | into, not | inside, independence |
| *non-* | not | nonfiction |
| *pre-* | before | prehistoric |
| *re-* | again | resend |
| *tele-* | far | telescope |
| *trans-* | across | transportation |
| *tri-* | three | triangle |
| *uni-* | one | unify |

## Suffixes

Suffixes are letter groups added after a base word to change or add to the word's meaning.

| Suffix | Meaning | Example |
| --- | --- | --- |
| *-er* | one who | teacher |
| *-er* | more | brighter |
| *-est* | most | brightest |
| *-ful* | full of | wonderful |
| *-ing* | (present tense) | smiling |
| *-less* | without | penniless |
| *-ling* | small | duckling |
| *-ly* | every | weekly |
| *-ly* | (adverb) | quickly |
| *-ness* | state of being | happiness |
| *-or* | one who | actor |
| *-y* | state of | funny |

# A Special Forest

**Read the passage below. Think about the meanings of the words in dark print.**

---

You are in a forest. It is so dark you can barely see the tree trunks around you. Few plants grow in the ground, so it is easy to walk around. You can hear monkeys high above you. You're in a **rain forest**!

A rain forest can be found somewhere that is warm and wet all year. The trees in the rain forest are always green. Some have beautiful flowers. **Fruit** grows on other trees. The fruit is food for the many animals in the rain forest. Some animals in the rain forest live their whole lives in the tops of the trees.

The trees in the rain forest are different **sizes**. Some are very tall, while others are shorter. Because of this, rain forests have several **levels**. The taller trees **form** the forest roof. The tops of shorter trees make a lower level. All the levels of tree **branches** keep light from getting to the forest floor.

Today the rain forests are in **danger**. People cut down the trees. **Pollution** kills the trees. If we don't work hard to save the rain forests, they might be lost forever.

**Go back to the passage. Underline the words or sentences that give you a clue to the meaning of each word in dark print.**


      Vocabulary in Context G2, SV 9780547625751

# Context Clues

**Read each sentence. Look for clues to help you finish each sentence
with a word from the box. Write the word on the line.**

| | | | |
|---|---|---|---|
| pollution | danger | fruit | levels |
| rain forest | branches | form | sizes |



**1.** A _________________ can be found somewhere that is warm and
wet all year.

**2.** Animals of many _________________ live in the rain forest.

**3.** The animals live on the different _________________ of the
rain forest.

**4.** Some walk and sleep on the _________________ of the trees.

**5.** They eat _________________ from the trees.

**6.** The tops of the trees _________________ a kind of umbrella.

**7.** Things people do, such as driving cars, can cause
_________________.

**8.** Rain forests are in _________________ because people keep cutting
down the trees.

# Dictionary Skills

Guide words are the two words at the top of each dictionary page. They show the first and last words on a page. All the words in between are in ABC order. Write the word from the box that would go on each page. Add a word that you know to each page.

branches   levels   fruit   pollution   danger



**1. apple/can**

_______________________________________________

_______________________________________________

**2. car/early**

_______________________________________________

_______________________________________________

**3. egg/good**

_______________________________________________

_______________________________________________

**4. keep/move**

_______________________________________________

_______________________________________________

**5. open/ran**

_______________________________________________

_______________________________________________

# Standardized Test Practice

**Read each sentence. Pick the word that best completes the sentence.
Circle the letter for the correct word.**

> **TIP**
> If you are not sure which word finishes the sentence, do the best
> you can. Try to choose the answer that makes the most sense.

Vocabulary in Context

**1.** A food that tastes sweet and grows on trees is ____.

  **A** paste      **C** shirts

  **B** fruit      **D** candy

**2.** A very thick forest that grows where it is warm and wet is a ____.

  **A** dry forest      **C** rain forest

  **B** cold forest      **D** snow forest

**3.** To tell how big things are, use ____.

  **A** sizes      **C** dresses

  **B** schools      **D** forks

**4.** Something high and something low are on different ____.

  **A** paths      **C** levels

  **B** rivers      **D** cars

**5.** To make is to ____.

  **A** break      **C** lift

  **B** wash      **D** form

**6.** The parts of a tree that grow out from its trunk are ____.

  **A** branches      **C** apples

  **B** leaves      **D** oranges

**7.** Something that can hurt you is a ____.

  **A** hope      **C** danger

  **B** help      **D** thought

**8.** Something people do to hurt the earth is called ____.

  **A** plants      **C** water

  **B** pollution      **D** air

# Related Words

The rain forest is full of all kinds of sounds. These words are related because they all name sounds.

| bellow   croak   hoot   warble   yowl |
|:---:|

**For boxes 1–5, read the sentence and draw a picture of an animal that makes the sound. For box 6, draw a picture showing when you might make one of the sounds.**

| | |
|---|---|
| **1.** A <u>bellow</u> is deep and roaring. | **4.** A <u>croak</u> is low and hoarse. |
| **2.** A <u>hoot</u> is a kind of cry. | **5.** A <u>warble</u> is song-like. |
| **3.** A <u>yowl</u> is a kind of whine. | **6.** I can _________________. |

**Word Skills**





Unit 1
Vocabulary in Context G2, SV 9780547625751

# Onomatopoeia

There are many words that describe sounds.

| bellow   croak   hoot   warble   yowl |

**Read the sound words in the box above. Write the words in the categories below. Add other words to complete each category.**

| LOUD SOUNDS | QUIET SOUNDS | GRUFF SOUNDS |
|---|---|---|
| **1.** bang | **3.** hush | **5.** grunt |
| | | |

| ANIMAL SOUNDS | WEATHER SOUNDS | MUSIC SOUNDS |
|---|---|---|
| **2.** yowl | **4.** whoosh | **6.** toot-toot |
| | | |

Word Skills



Vocabulary in Context G2, SV 9780547625751

# Descriptive Words

Which words are more descriptive? Why?

"Hurray," Mitchell said.          "Ouch," Joan said.
"Hurray," Mitchell bellowed.      "Ouch," Joan yowled.

**Substitute another word for said. Write the word on the line. Draw a picture to illustrate the sentence. Share your ideas with classmates.**

| | |
|---|---|
| **1.** "Let's play ball," said Juan. | **4.** "I'm late," said Meg. |
| **2.** "What time is it?" said Raj. | **5.** "Help, help!" said Sy. |
| **3.** "Oink, oink," said the pig. | **6.** "Grrr, grrr," said the bear. |

Word Skills

# Word Search

| pollution | danger | fruit | levels | rain forest |
|-----------|--------|-------|--------|-------------|
| branches | form | sizes | bellow | croak |
| hoot | warble | yowl | | |

## Make a word search. Follow these steps:

**1.** Read the vocabulary words in the box above.

**2.** Write the vocabulary words in the puzzle below. Write the words across in rows and up and down in columns.

**3.** Some of the words may crisscross. Others may not.

**4.** Fill in the rest of the puzzle with other letters.

| | | f | | | | | | y |
|---|---|---|---|---|---|---|---|---|
| | h | o | o | t | | | | o |
| | | r | | | | | | w |
| | | m | | | | | | l |
| | | | | | | | | |
| | | | | | | | | |
| | | | | | | | | |
| | | | | | | | | |
| | | | | | | | | |
| | | | | | | | | |







Word Skills

# Draw and Label

Draw a picture of a rain forest below. Then use the words in the box to label things you drew in your picture. Use as many words as you can.

| | | | | |
|---|---|---|---|---|
| pollution | danger | fruit | levels | rain forest |
| branches | form | sizes | bellow | croak |
| hoot | warble | yowl | | |

Word Skills

# Writing

Imagine you just visited a rain forest. What plants and animals did you see? What sounds did you hear?

**On the lines below, write to a friend about your trip to the rain forest. Use some vocabulary words from this unit in your writing.**

_______________________

(date)

Dear Friend,

_______________________________________________

_______________________________________________

_______________________________________________

_______________________________________________

_______________________________________________

_______________________________________________

_______________________________________________

Your friend,

_______________________



Writing

# In the Fields

**Read the passage below. Think about the meanings of the words in dark print.**

---

A bird flies high above the cornfield. The **tractor** begins to hum. The farmer drives the tractor toward the long rows of corn. As he begins to pick the corn, long-eared rabbits run for safety. The farmer is happy. He is ready to pick all the **grain** he grew this year. Another **harvest** has begun!

At harvest time in the fall, the colors in the fields change. Then the farmer picks the corn. Next he picks oats and wheat. During the harvest, the farmer works very hard and gets much **exercise**. He will need plenty of **rest** at night. He must have a good **diet** and plenty of the best foods. He will need enough **energy** to load all the grain onto a truck. The farmer will use the truck to take the grain to the market.

The grain will be used in many foods. The wheat, corn, and oats will be used to make bread and cereal. These foods are part of a **healthy** diet.

The farmer feels proud. He knows many people will enjoy the food from his harvest.

**Go back to the passage. Underline the words or sentences that give you a clue to the meaning of each word in dark print.**

Vocabulary in Context G2, SV 9780547625751

# Context Clues

**Meanings for the vocabulary words are given below. Go back to the passage and read each sentence that has a vocabulary word. If you still cannot tell the meaning, look for clues in the sentences that come before and after the one with the vocabulary word. Write each word from the box in front of its meaning.**

| | | | |
|---|---|---|---|
| diet | tractor | harvest | exercise |
| rest | grain | energy | healthy |

1. _________________ : wheat, oats, and corn

2. _________________ : a machine used on a farm

3. _________________ : the foods a person eats every day

4. _________________ : the picking of crops

5. _________________ : good for the body

6. _________________ : sleep

7. _________________ : the power of work

8. _________________ : moving of the body in work or play

Unit 2
Vocabulary in Context G2, SV 9780547625751

Vocabulary in Context

# Dictionary Skills

**Synonyms are words that have the same or almost the same meaning. Read each sentence. Circle the word or words in each sentence that are a synonym for the word in dark print.**



tractor **1.** Tom drives his farm machine almost every day.

harvest **2.** He uses the tractor for the picking of crops.

diet **3.** He also makes sure he eats good food every day.

exercise **4.** All this work keeps him in shape.

rest **5.** Tom makes sure he gets all the sleep he needs.

energy **6.** He has the power to work because he has a good diet.

grain **7.** He eats cereal made of wheat, oats, and corn.

healthy **8.** Tom is not sick very often because he does all these things.

# Relating Words

**Answer the questions below. Use the passage on page 18 for help.**

**1.** Why would farmers find it useful to have a **tractor**?

_______________________________________________

**2.** What happens at **harvest** time in the fall?

_______________________________________________

# Crossword Puzzle

Use the clues and the words in the box to finish the crossword puzzle.

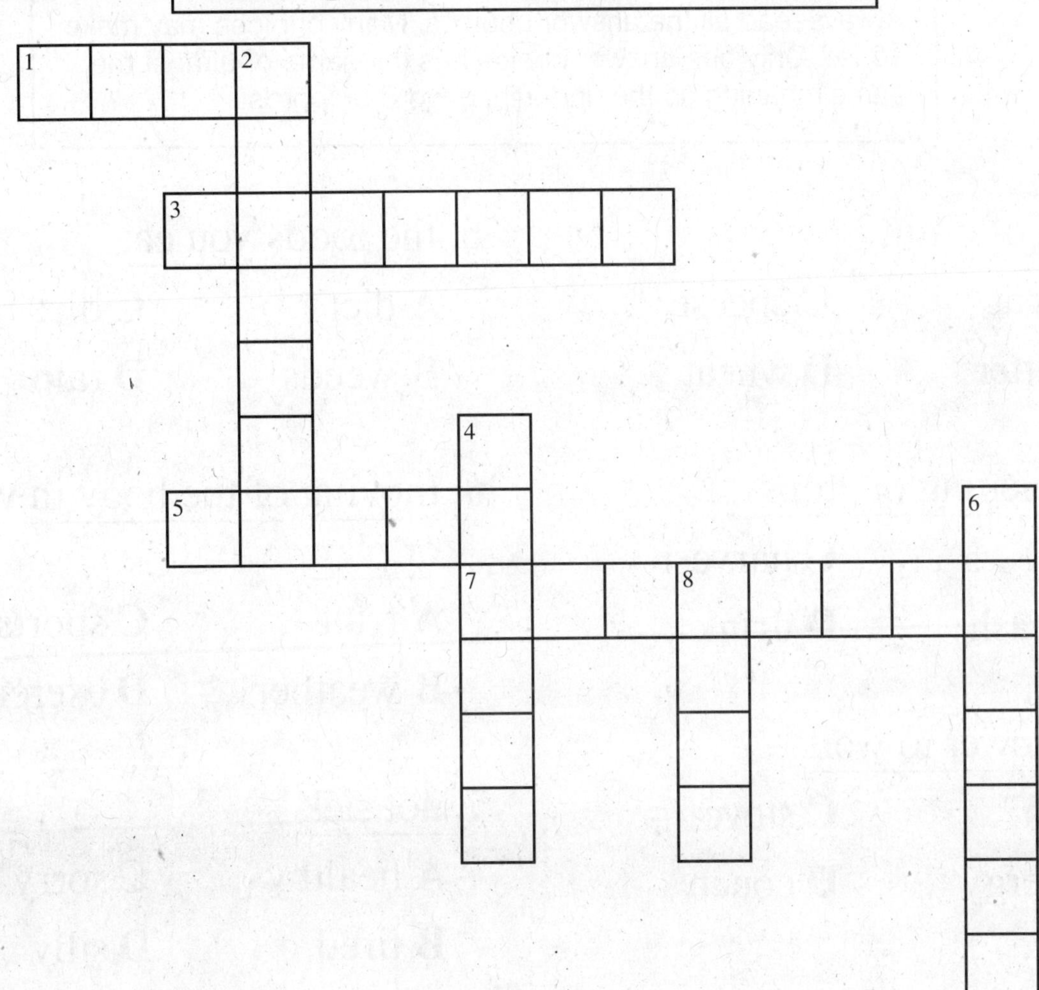





## Across

**1.** the foods a person eats every day

**3.** the picking of crops

**5.** wheat, oats, and corn

**7.** moving of the body in work or play

## Down

**2.** a machine used on a farm

**4.** the power to work

**6.** not sick

**8.** sleep

# Standardized Test Practice

**Look for the word that has the same or almost the same meaning as the underlined word or words. Circle the letter beside your choice.**

**TIP**

> Always read all the answer choices. Many choices may make sense. Only one answer choice has the same or almost the same meaning as the underlined word or words.

**1.** kind of <u>grain</u>

  **A** meat      **C** cheese

  **B** butter      **D** wheat

**2.** the <u>picking of crops</u>

  **A** trip      **C** harvest

  **B** smash      **D** drink

**3.** the <u>power to work</u>

  **A** fun      **C** stove

  **B** energy      **D** couch

**4.** get some <u>rest</u>

  **A** books      **C** sleep

  **B** birds      **D** teeth

**5.** the <u>foods you eat</u>

  **A** diet      **C** dirt

  **B** weeds      **D** rain

**6.** <u>moving of the body in work or play</u>

  **A** fruit      **C** sports

  **B** weather      **D** exercise

**7.** <u>not sick</u>

  **A** healthy      **C** sorry

  **B** tired      **D** silly

**8.** <u>machine</u> on a farm

  **A** bus      **C** train

  **B** plane      **D** tractor

## Content-Area Words

You would probably find all of these words in a book about the sea.

salt     water     fish     waves     tides     shells     shore

**Think about the words you might find in a book about farms. Fill in the word web below. Use words from the box. Add other words.**

| | | | | |
|---|---|---|---|---|
| **field** | **sidewalk** | **pasture** | **farmland** | **skyscraper** |
| **desk** | **airport** | **meadow** | **gym** | **countryside** |

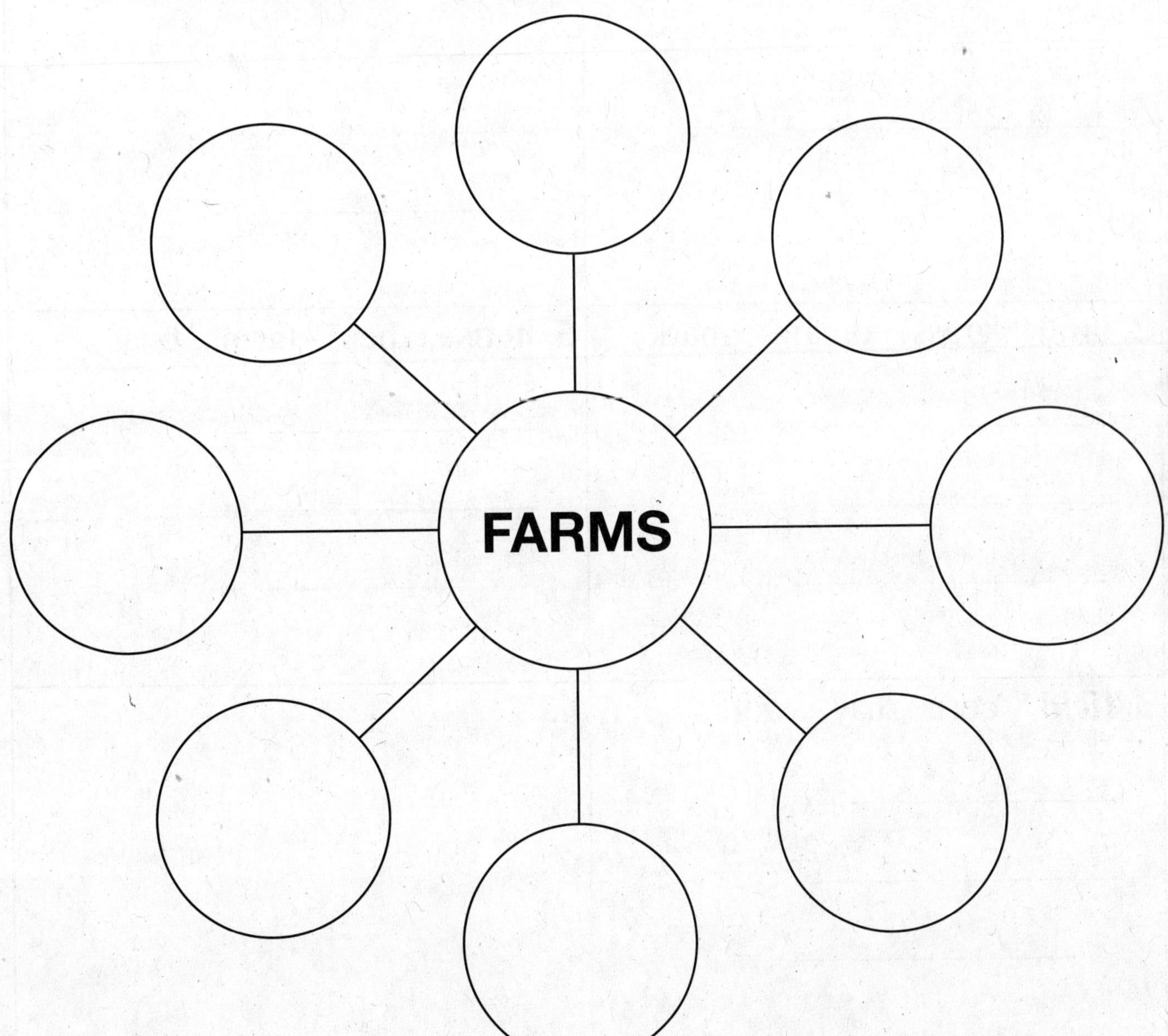






Unit 2
Vocabulary in Context G2, SV 9780547625751

# Compound Words

A compound word is made by putting two words together.

country + side = countryside

**Join the word in dark print with the other words to make compound words. In the last box, draw and label a picture for one of the words you wrote. The first word is written for you.**

<table>
<tr><td>

**1. side**   in   out   walk

inside
_______________

_______________

_______________

</td><td>

**4. yard**   back   farm   stick

_______________

_______________

_______________

</td></tr>
<tr><td>

**2. land**   grass   dream   mark

_______________

_______________

_______________

</td><td>

**5. house**   hen   farm   boat

_______________

_______________

_______________

</td></tr>
<tr><td>

**3. field**   corn   hay   work

_______________

_______________

_______________

</td><td>

**6.**

</td></tr>
</table>





Unit 2
Vocabulary in Context G2, SV 9780547625751

# Analogies

Look at each word puzzle. Think about why the words go together.

| | | |
|---|---|---|
| **big–large** | **up–down** | **round–ball** |
| **hot–warm** | **city–country** | **square–box** |

Big and large have similar meanings. Why does warm belong with hot?

Up and down are opposites. Why does country belong with city?

A ball is round. Why does box belong with square?

**Complete the word puzzles. Think about why the first two words go together. Write a word that goes with the third word in the same way. Use the words in the box below to help you.**

| | | | | | |
|---|---|---|---|---|---|
| **gardener** | **cow** | **sad** | **small** | **bird** | **sand** |

**1.** shiny–bright

little–_______________

**4.** no–yes

happy–_______________

**2.** kitten–cat

calf–_______________

**5.** farm–farmer

garden–_______________

**3.** pasture–grass

desert–_______________

**6.** gallop–horse

fly–_______________

**Word Skills**




**25**

Unit 2
Vocabulary in Context G2, SV 9780547625751

# Adding -<u>ed</u> and -<u>ing</u>

When you add **-<u>ed</u>** to an action word, you are usually talking about something that happened yesterday or long ago. When you add **-<u>ing</u>**, you are describing something that is happening now.

**Then**   pick + **ed** = pick**ed**
**Now**   pick + **ing** = pick**ing**

**Write a paragraph about farmers picking and bringing their crops to market long ago or today. Use one of the forms of pick above.**

_______________________________________________

_______________________________________________

_______________________________________________

_______________________________________________

_______________________________________________

# Picture Cards

**Draw a picture of each word below.**

**1.** pasture

**2.** countryside

Name _________________________________________________ Date _______________

# Writing

Farming is hard work. Farmers do chores every day. Just like the farmers, you do many things every day.

**On the lines below, tell about the things you do every day. Tell why you do these things. Use some vocabulary words from this unit in your writing.**

__________________________________________________________________________

__________________________________________________________________________

__________________________________________________________________________

__________________________________________________________________________

__________________________________________________________________________

__________________________________________________________________________

__________________________________________________________________________

__________________________________________________________________________

__________________________________________________________________________

__________________________________________________________________________

**Writing**





Vocabulary in Context G2, SV 9780547625751

# A House Built of Sticks

**Read the passage below. Think about the meanings of the words in dark print.**

---

People live in homes built by **carpenters**. The carpenters use tools to build these homes. But animals are different. Many live in trees or in caves. But **beavers** are animals that build very special homes.

A beaver's home is called a **lodge**. It is built in a pond or a lake. This lodge is made from sticks and mud. There is a **cozy** room inside where the beaver lives. This room is above the water and stays warm and dry. The lodge protects the beaver from the cold. The beaver is safe from its **enemies** because the only door to its lodge is under the water. The beaver swims under the water and climbs up into the lodge.

Sometimes the beaver cannot find a pond or a lake. So it builds a **dam** across a stream. The beaver cuts down trees with its teeth. Then it uses the trees, sticks, and mud to make a dam. The dam **blocks** the water to make a pond for the beaver's lodge.

Beavers build **amazing** homes. Maybe someday you will get to see a beaver home.

**Go back to the passage. Underline the words or sentences that give you a clue to the meaning of each word in dark print.**

Vocabulary in Context G2, SV 9780547625751

# Context Clues

**Read each sentence. Look for clues to help you finish each sentence with a word from the box. Write the word on the line.**

| | | | |
|---|---|---|---|
| **lodge** | **beavers** | **cozy** | **carpenters** |
| **blocks** | **enemies** | **dam** | **amazing** |

1. People who build houses are called ________________.

2. ________________ cut down trees with their teeth to build their homes.

3. A beaver home is called a ________________.

4. A beaver home feels ________________ on a cold lake.

5. Beavers are safe from their ________________ in their homes.

6. A beaver home is an ________________ sight!

7. A beaver ________________ water in a stream to make a pond.

8. Beavers build a ________________ across the stream.

Vocabulary in Context G2, SV 9780547625751

# Cloze Paragraphs

**Use words in the box to finish the paragraphs. Read the
paragraphs again to be sure they make sense.**

| | | | |
|---|---|---|---|
| lodge | beavers | cozy | carpenters |
| blocks | enemies | dam | amazing |

There are (1) _______________ who have jobs building homes for

people. But (2) _______________ are animals that build their own

homes. The homes they build look (3) _______________! A beaver

home is called a (4) _______________. A beaver builds this lodge out

of sticks and mud. The room inside the lodge is (5) _______________

and dry. The lodge keeps the beaver warm and protects it from its

(6) _______________.

What happens when a beaver cannot find a pond or a lake? Then

it makes a pond! The beaver (7) _______________ a stream with

sticks, logs, and mud. This is called a (8) _______________. Then the

beaver can build its lodge.

# Word Groups

**Read each pair of words. Think about how they are alike. Write the word from the box that belongs in each word group.**

| | | | |
|---|---|---|---|
| lodge | beavers | cozy | carpenters |
| blocks | enemies | dam | amazing |

**1.** bridge, wall, _______________________________

**2.** mice, squirrels, _______________________________

**3.** nails, saws, _______________________________

**4.** warm, soft, _______________________________

**5.** surprising, wonderful, _______________________________

**6.** stops, ends, _______________________________

**7.** house, room, _______________________________

**8.** hunters, attackers, _______________________________

# Dictionary Skills

**Look at the words in the group. Write them on the lines in ABC order.**

**1.** carpenter _______________________  **2.** lodge _______________________

home _______________________  water _______________________

tools _______________________  mud _______________________

build _______________________  dry _______________________


 Vocabulary in Context G2, SV 9780547625751

# Standardized Test Practice

**Read each sentence. Pick the word that best completes the sentence. Circle the letter for the correct word.**

Read carefully. Use the other words in the sentence to help you choose each missing word.



**1.** _____ are animals that build their own homes.

  **A** Beavers      **C** Dogs

  **B** Cats      **D** Bears

**2.** A beaver home is called a _____.

  **A** house      **C** room

  **B** lodge      **D** cave

**3.** A beaver home is an _____ sight.

  **A** amazing      **C** easy

  **B** ugly      **D** open

**4.** A _____ is made of sticks, logs, and mud.

  **A** pond      **C** dam

  **B** tree      **D** ground

**5.** A dam _____ water to make a pond.

  **A** lets      **C** blocks

  **B** freezes      **D** sees

**6.** People live in homes built by _____.

  **A** beavers      **C** animals

  **B** children      **D** carpenters

**7.** A beaver home is _____ and warm.

  **A** cozy      **C** cold

  **B** hard      **D** lost

**8.** The home under the water helps protect beavers from their _____.

  **A** babies      **C** friends

  **B** enemies      **D** brothers

# Using Context

Context means "the way in which a word is used." What context clues
help you understand the meaning of the underlined words?

Some animals dig underground homes called burrows.

The words animals, dig, and underground homes help you understand
that burrows are "underground homes."

**Answer each question by circling the letter beside the best answer.**

1. The mother fox takes food to her babies in their safe lair.
   What clues help you understand that a lair is a home?

   **A** the, to, her

   **B** food, babies, safe

2. All those chickens have a roost in that big henhouse.
   What clues help you understand that chickens perch on a roost?

   **A** all, that, big

   **B** chickens, henhouse

3. The beavers used sticks, twigs, and leaves to build their lodge.
   What clues help you understand how beavers make a lodge?

   **A** sticks, twigs, leaves, build

   **B** used, and, leaves

4. The opening in the side of the hill leads to a bear's cave.
   What clues help you understand that a cave is underground?

   **A** opening, side of the hill

   **B** side, leads to a

**Word Skills**

# Multiple-Meaning Words

Many words have more than one meaning.

An animal's underground home is called a <u>burrow</u>.
I'm going to <u>burrow</u> under the blanket to get warm.

**All of the underlined words can name animal homes. Draw a picture to show another meaning for each underlined word.**

| | |
|---|---|
| **1.** I'm so tired! Let's stop and <u>roost</u> on this bench. | **3.** Joe cleared the snow off the roof. He was afraid the roof might <u>cave</u> in. |
| **2.** The pirates hid the stolen treasure in their secret <u>lair</u>. No one could find it. | **4.** When we went to the beach, we stayed at the Seaside <u>Lodge</u>. |





Word Skills

Unit 3
Vocabulary in Context G2, SV 9780547625751

# Content-Area Words

**The words in the box name different kinds of homes. Use these words when you follow the directions in boxes 1 and 2 below.**

| | | | | |
|---|---|---|---|---|
| cottage | lair | apartment | lodge | house |
| burrow | cave | roost | cabin | tent |

## 1. ANIMALS' HOMES

You would learn about animals' homes in science class. List animals' homes here.

## 3. PEOPLE'S HOMES

You would learn about people's homes in social studies class. List people's homes here.

## 2. OTHER SCIENCE WORDS

Write other science words you know.

## 4. OTHER SOCIAL STUDIES WORDS

Write other social studies words you know.

Word Skills

# Riddles

**Choose the word from the box that answers each riddle.**
**Write your answers on the lines.**

| castle   ranch   cabin   cave   house |
| --- |

**1.** I can be small and made of logs. _______________

**2.** I am a building where people live. _______________

**3.** I am home to bats and lizards. _______________

**4.** I am a home for a king. _______________

**5.** I am a place where animals are raised. _______________

# Words with -ed and -ing

The naming words **ranch** and **lodge** can also be used to show action.

| The cowboy will **ranch** for the rest of his life.<br>My family plans to **lodge** at the inn next summer. |
| --- |

**Add -ed and -ing to the words ranch and lodge as shown below.**
**Use each word in a sentence.**

| ranch + **ed** = ranch**ed**     lodge + **ed** = lodg**ed**<br>ranch + **ing** = ranch**ing**     lodge + **ing** = lodg**ing** |
| --- |

**1.** _______________________________________________

**2.** _______________________________________________

**3.** _______________________________________________

**4.** _______________________________________________



**36**

# Writing

People live in many different kinds of homes. Pretend that you are building your own home. Where will you build it? What is it made of? Who will live with you?

**On the lines below, write a story telling about your home. Use some vocabulary words from this unit in your writing.**

_______________________________________________

_______________________________________________

_______________________________________________

_______________________________________________

_______________________________________________

_______________________________________________

_______________________________________________

_______________________________________________

_______________________________________________





Writing

# Riding into Space

**Read the passage below. Think about the meanings of the words in dark print.**

---

When Sally Ride was a child, she wanted to be an **astronaut**. She dreamed of flying into space. Sally didn't think her dream would come true. At that time, all the American astronauts were men.

When Sally grew up, she **studied** to learn about the stars. She also studied **planets**, such as Earth. One day Sally read in the newspaper that new astronauts were needed. Sally wrote a letter, and she was picked.

Sally needed many hours of **training** to learn to be an astronaut. She learned what to do during the **flight** into space. At last Sally flew on the **shuttle** *Challenger*, a spaceship with wings. Sally helped put **satellites** into space to go around Earth. These machines sent pictures to Earth. She also did many **experiments** to find out about things in space.

Sally was the first American woman to travel in space. Most people think she is special because of this. Sally doesn't think she is any more important than the other astronauts.

**Go back to the passage. Underline the words or sentences that give you a clue to the meaning of each word in dark print.**

## Context Clues

**Read each sentence. Look for clues to help you finish each sentence with a word from the box. Write the correct word on the line.**

| | | |
|---|---|---|
| experiments | satellites | studied |
| astronaut | training | planets |

1. An _______________ is someone who flies into space.

2. Astronauts need much _______________.

3. They must do _______________ to learn how things happen.

4. They must know how _______________ can send pictures back to Earth.

5. Sally Ride _______________ hard to become an astronaut.

6. She knows about many _______________, including Earth.

## Class Survey

**Complete the chart below. Write your own questions using three of the vocabulary words. Poll your classmates. Use tallies to mark your results.**

| Question | Yes | No |
|---|---|---|
| Can you name one **astronaut?** | | |
| | | |
| | | |
| | | |







Vocabulary in Context

# Word Groups

**Read each pair of words. Think about how they are alike. Write the word from the box that best finishes each word group.**

| experiments | satellites | studied | shuttle |
|---|---|---|---|
| astronaut | training | planets | flight |

**1.** teacher, doctor, _______________________

**2.** fly, flying, _______________________

**3.** moon, stars, _______________________

**4.** airplane, spaceship, _______________________

**5.** thought, read, _______________________

**6.** teaching, learning, _______________________

**7.** tests, tries, _______________________

**8.** machines, pictures, _______________________

# Word Codes

A code is a kind of secret writing. Each letter stands for a different letter.

**Use the box at the bottom of the page to find each coded word. Write your answers on the lines above the letters.**

| experiments | planets |
| astronaut | shuttle |

**1.** __ __ __ __ __ __ __
   k  o  z  m  v  g  h

bodies in space that move around the sun

**2.** __ __ __ __ __ __ __ __ __
   z  h  g  i  l  m  z  f  g

a person who flies into space

**3.** __ __ __ __ __ __ __
   h  s  f  g  g  o  v

a spaceship with wings that can be used many times

**4.** __ __ __ __ __ __ __ __ __ __ __
   v  c  k  v  i  r  n  v  m  g  h

tests to find out something

| a=z | b=y | c=x | d=w | e=v | f=u | g=t |
| h=s | i=r | j=q | k=p | l=o | m=n | n=m |
| o=l | p=k | q=j | r=i | s=h | t=g | u=f |
| v=e | w=d | x=c | y=b | z=a | | |

# Standardized Test Practice

**Read each sentence. Pick the word that best completes the sentence. Circle the letter for the correct word.**

**TIP**

Use each answer choice in place of the underlined word or words. Remember that the underlined word or words and your answer must have the same meaning.



**1.** A person who flies into space is an _____.

A actor      C airplane

B author      D astronaut

**2.** If you tried to learn, you _____.

A laughed      C studied

B played      D jumped

**3.** Round bodies in space are _____.

A balls      C trains

B cars      D planets

**4.** The act of flying is called _____.

A class      C school

B flight      D thought

**5.** A spaceship with wings is a _____.

A person      C shuttle

B road      D wagon

**6.** Machines in space are _____.

A satellites      C moons

B stars      D clouds

**7.** Teaching someone to do something is _____.

A saying      C sitting

B training      D thinking

**8.** Tests to find out something are _____.

A experiments      C trucks

B animals      D planes

# Using Context

What word in the sentence below helps you understand the meaning of <u>revolving</u>?

Earth is <u>revolving</u> around the sun.

The word <u>around</u> helps you understand that <u>revolving</u> means "going around."

**The word <u>around</u> can help you understand the meaning of other words. Read each sentence. Draw a picture to show the meaning of the underlined word.**

| | |
|---|---|
| **1.** The moon's path around Earth is called an <u>orbit</u>. | **3.** The dancer is <u>spinning</u> around on one foot! |
| **2.** We walked around in a <u>circular</u> path. | **4.** If I twist a string around my finger, I can make a <u>spiral</u>. |

Word Skills

# Word Families

A word family is a group of words that are related. Find the word
revolving in this word ladder.

> **revolve**
> **revolves**
> **revolved**
> **revolving**
> **revolution**

## Add another word to each of the following word families.

| | |
|---|---|
| **1.** blast<br>blasts<br>blasted<br>______________________ | **5.** spin<br>spins<br>spinner<br>______________________ |
| **2.** spiral<br>spirals<br>spiraled<br>______________________ | **6.** orb<br>orbit<br>orbits<br>______________________ |
| **3.** center<br>central<br>centered<br>______________________ | **7.** cloud<br>clouds<br>clouded<br>______________________ |
| **4.** sun<br>sunny<br>sunnier<br>______________________ | **8.** star<br>starry<br>starfish<br>______________________ |

Word Skills



Vocabulary in Context G2, SV 9780547625751

# Multiple-Meaning Words

Many words have different meanings.

The planets are <u>revolving</u> around the sun.
Be careful when you walk through a <u>revolving</u> door.

**Read the sentences. Think about the meaning of the underlined word or words. Circle the letter that tells what the underlined word or words mean.**

**1.** Sandy fixed her hair in <u>spiral</u> curls.

A  a circular shape

B  a square shape

C  a triangle shape

**2.** The toy top is <u>spinning</u> faster and faster.

A  flying

B  turning

C  jumping

**3.** To write an *o*, you make a <u>circle</u>.

A  round shape

B  square shape

C  straight line

**4.** Don't let the noise <u>spiral out of control</u>!

A  spin in circles

B  turn into a circular shape

C  grow too loud

**5.** It's fun to listen when Gramps starts <u>spinning</u> a story.

A  dropping

B  turning pages in

C  making up

**6.** Seth and I have the same <u>circle of friends</u>.

A  friends who draw circles

B  group of friends

C  round-shaped friends

Word Skills

# Draw and Label

Draw a picture of outer space below. Then use the words in the box to label things you drew in your picture. Include as many words as you can.

| | | | | |
|---|---|---|---|---|
| experiments | satellites | studied | shuttle | astronaut |
| training | planets | flight | revolve | spin |
| orbit | circle | spiral | | |

# Writing

Sally Ride wanted to be an astronaut when she grew up. She had to work very hard to become an astronaut.

**On the lines below, tell what you want to do in the future. Tell why you want to do this. Tell if you will need special training. Use some vocabulary words from this unit in your writing.**

____________________________________________

____________________________________________

____________________________________________

____________________________________________

____________________________________________

____________________________________________

____________________________________________

____________________________________________





Unit 4
Vocabulary in Context G2, SV 9780547625751

Writing

# Dragons in the Street

**Read the story. Think about the meanings of the words in dark print.**

---

"It is time to go to the parade," said Chen.

"Why are we going outside when it is so cold?" asked John, Chen's best friend.

"Because it is Chinese New Year!" Chen answered. "This year, the Chinese New Year begins on February 10. At least it isn't raining!"

"I don't want to see the dragon parade," John said.

"Why not?" Chen asked. "It will be fun!

"Dragons **frighten** me!" John said. "I get scared."

"No, no," said Chen. "Dragons are strong and good! They bring us good luck!"

Chen handed John a bright red apple. "Red is the color of good luck. On New Year's Day, we wear good clothes, think good thoughts, and say only kind words. That way, we will have good luck all year!"

John looked around. He saw red **decorations** everywhere. "Does everyone have red for good luck?" he asked.

Chen nodded. She was carrying gifts wrapped in red for her friends.

Vocabulary in Context G2, SV 9780547625751

"See here," she said. "I have little red **envelopes** sealed with a little money inside. These are for my cousins so that they will have good luck in the new year."

"I don't want to watch the parade!" John said.

"Why not?" Chen asked. "Remember last year when the lion dancers jumped and **pounced**! Wasn't it fun?"

"Yes," John agreed. "But now the sharp noise of all the **firecrackers** hurts my ears."

"That's because they are **celebrating**! It's like one big party!" Chen shouted over the noise, "Come on!"

Men holding long poles weaved and ran through the street. They held a long dragon like a green and gold snake on the poles above their heads. The men **pranced** from side to side. The dragon swept up and down. The dragon was red, green, and gold.

"It's beautiful!" John cried.

"Yes," Chen answered. "Now that the dragon has passed, we will have a **banquet**. Everyone will eat together."

"I feel so silly!" John said. "Why was I afraid of the dragon? The dragon gives good luck to all of us! Now, let's go eat!"

**Go back to the story. Underline the words or sentences that give you a clue to the meaning of each word in dark print.**

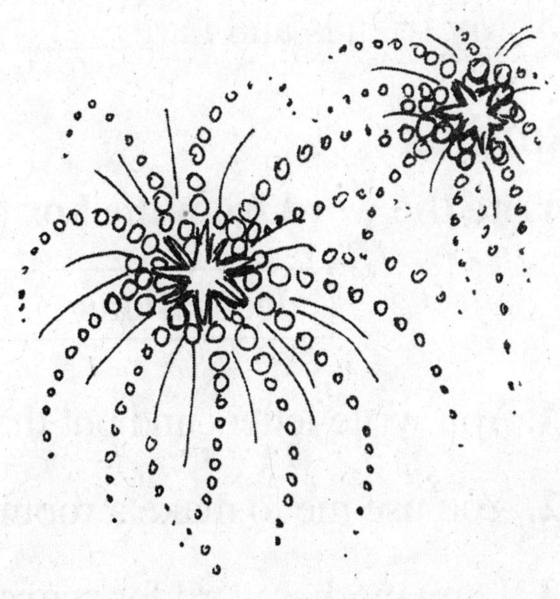

Name _______________________________  Date _______________________

# Context Clues

**Read each sentence. Look for clues to help you finish each sentence with a word from the box. Write the word on the line.**

| | | | |
|---|---|---|---|
| pranced | firecrackers | banquet | frighten |
| pounced | decorations | envelopes | celebrating |

1. We hung colorful ____________________ before the party.

2. The children opened the paper ____________________ to see what was inside.

3. The horse ____________________ during the whole parade.

4. The bears at the zoo ____________________ me.

5. Everyone ate wonderful food at the Thanksgiving

   ____________________.

6. The ____________________ made a loud noise.

7. The lion ____________________ on the mouse.

8. My friends and I are ____________________ the beginning of summer.

# Riddles

**Write the word from the box that answers each riddle.**

| | | |
|---|---|---|
| decorations | frighten | envelopes |

1. You write letters and put them inside me. ____________________

2. You use me to make a room look special. ____________________

3. I am another word for **scare**. ____________________

# Classifying

**Study each group of words. Think about how they are alike. Then finish each group with a word from the box. Add another word that you know to each group.**

Vocabulary in Context

| decorations | pounced |
|---|---|
| banquet | firecrackers |

**1. Times to Eat**
picnic
cookout

_________________________

_________________________

**2. Fireworks**
sparklers

_________________________

_________________________

**3. Ways Lion Dancers Moved**
spun
jumped

_________________________

_________________________

**4. _________________________**
balloons
ribbons
colored lights

_________________________

# Standardized Test Practice

**Read each sentence. Pick the word that best completes the sentence. Circle the letter for the correct word.**

**TIP** Read each sentence carefully. Use the other words in the sentences to help you choose each missing word.

**1.** The cat ____ on the toy.
  **A** scared     **C** pounced
  **B** answered   **D** gave

**2.** The letters came in white ____.
  **A** cars    **C** animals
  **B** plates  **D** envelopes

**3.** They hung ____ for the birthday party.
  **A** clothes       **C** books
  **B** decorations   **D** sailboats

**4.** Our family is ____ Mom's new job.
  **A** swimming   **C** celebrating
  **B** confusing  **D** painting

**5.** The loud noises ____ me!
  **A** frighten  **C** collect
  **B** jump      **D** tumble

**6.** We lit ____ on the Fourth of July.
  **A** firecrackers  **C** movies
  **B** beaches       **D** trees

**7.** The pony ____ at the head of the parade.
  **A** crawled  **C** swam
  **B** pranced  **D** laughed

**8.** Everyone went to a big ____ to eat good food.
  **A** game   **C** flower
  **B** money  **D** banquet





Unit 5
Vocabulary in Context G2, SV 9780547625751

# Synonyms

A parade is full of all kinds of movement. These words are synonyms.
They have similar meanings.

| coil   swirl   twirl   twist   whirl |

**Draw pictures to illustrate the sentences.**

| **1.** The rattlesnake is <u>coiled</u>. | **4.** The bee <u>swirls</u> around the flower. |
| **2.** I can <u>twirl</u> this stick. | **5.** I can <u>twist</u> this rope to make a lasso. |
| **3.** When I dance, I like to <u>whirl</u>. | **6.** The chimney smoke <u>spirals</u> in the air. |

Word Skills

# Rhyming Words

Rhyming words end with the same sounds. They begin with different sounds.

–ot: <u>c</u>ot, <u>d</u>ot, <u>g</u>ot, <u>h</u>ot, <u>j</u>ot, <u>l</u>ot, <u>n</u>ot, <u>p</u>ot, <u>r</u>ot, <u>tr</u>ot, <u>bl</u>ot, <u>pl</u>ot, <u>sp</u>ot

**Write rhyming words for the phonograms in dark print. Start by using the letters in the ( ). Then use other letters.**

**1. –in** (sp)

___________________

___________________

___________________

**2. –ist** (tw)

___________________

___________________

___________________

**3. –urn** (t)

___________________

___________________

___________________

**4. –irl** (tw, wh, sw)

___________________

___________________

___________________

**5. –oil** (c)

___________________

___________________

___________________

**6. –ing** (r)

___________________

___________________

___________________





Unit 5
Vocabulary in Context G2, SV 9780547625751

Word Skills

# Blended Words

Sometimes two words have been blended to make another word.

twist + whirl = twirl          flash + glare = flare

## Draw pictures to show the meaning of the blended words.

| | |
|---|---|
| **1.** gleam + shimmer = glimmer | **3.** squirm + wiggle = squiggle |
| **2.** motor + pedal = moped | **4.** motor + hotel = motel |

Word Skills


    Vocabulary in Context G2, SV 9780547625751

# Word Search

| | |
|---|---|
| pranced     firecrackers     banquet     frighten     pounced | |
| decorations     envelopes     celebrating     coil     swirl | |
| twirl     twist     whirl | |

## Make a word search. Follow these steps:

1. Read the words in the box above.

2. Write the words in the puzzle below. Write the words across in rows and up and down in columns.

3. Some of the words may crisscross. Others may not.

4. Fill in the rest of the puzzle with other letters.

| | | | | | | | | | |
|---|---|---|---|---|---|---|---|---|---|
| | | | p | | | | | | t |
| | | | r | | | | | | w |
| | | | a | | | | | | i |
| p | o | u | n | c | e | d | | | r |
| | | | c | | | | | | l |
| | | | e | | | | | | |
| | | | d | | | | | | |
| | | | | | | | | | |
| | | | | | | | | | |
| | | | | | | | | | |





Unit 5
Vocabulary in Context G2, SV 9780547625751

# Writing

For Chen, New Year's Day is a special day. What special day is your favorite? What do you do on that day? Why do you like it? Do you go somewhere? Do you eat special foods? Do you see many people?

**Use the lines below to write about your special day. Use some vocabulary words from this unit in your writing.**

On my special day, I like to ___________________________________

________________________________________________

# What's in a Name?

**Read the story. Think about the meanings of the words in dark print.**

---

"Our school is named for Martin Luther King, Jr.," said Mr. Díaz. "Does anyone know why so many schools and roads are named for Martin Luther King, Jr.?"

That question made Marty think. His name was Martin, too.

"There is even a holiday for Martin Luther King, Jr. It is on the third Monday of January every year," the teacher said.

"It is because he had a great name!" Marty said. He felt **excited** because he and Martin Luther King, Jr., had the same first name.

Mr. Díaz laughed. "That may be," he said. "But our school was named for Martin Luther King, Jr., for the same reason that other schools and streets are named for George Washington and Abraham Lincoln."

"They were presidents," Angela said.

"Yes," said Tommy, "but there were other presidents."

"Tommy is right," Mr. Díaz said. "But George Washington and Abraham Lincoln were great men. They made things **change** in our country. So did Martin Luther King, Jr."

Mr. Díaz **described** how Martin Luther King, Jr., grew up in Atlanta, Georgia, in the 1930s. At the time, African American children could not go the same schools as white children. Even though they might be friends, African American and white children sometimes got in trouble for playing together. African American children could not eat in the same places as white children. They could not **join** the same clubs. They could not even drink from the same water fountains. They had to live **apart**.

All his life, Martin Luther King, Jr., had a **dream**. His dream was that someday people would all be equal. When African Americans and whites were not treated the same, he became **upset**. He wanted to do something about it.

But he was always **calm** as he worked for change. He worked hard to make the laws change. Thanks to his hard work, children today all can go to the same schools.

"Think about Martin Luther King, Jr., when you come to school in the morning," Mr. Díaz said. "He was brave. He worked to make the world a better place for everyone. He wanted to bring people together. How can you be like Martin Luther King, Jr.?"

**Go back to the story. Underline the words or sentences that give you a clue to the meaning of each word in dark print.**

Unit 6
Vocabulary in Context G2, SV 9780547625751

# Context Clues

**Meanings for the vocabulary words are given below. Go back to the story and read each sentence that has a vocabulary word. If you still cannot tell the meaning, look for clues in the sentences that come before and after the one with the vocabulary word. Write each word from the box in front of its meaning.**



1. ___________________: unhappy

2. ___________________: told about or written about

3. ___________________: not together

4. ___________________: very happy

5. ___________________: a wish

6. ___________________: come together with

7. ___________________: to become different

8. ___________________: quiet and still





Unit 6
Vocabulary in Context G2, SV 9780547625751

# Antonyms

Antonyms are words with opposite meanings.

**Circle the word or words in the sentence that are antonyms of the words in dark print.**

**upset**

1. Mike was happy that he could take his family to the fair.

**apart**

2. They always have a good time doing things together.

**calm**

3. When they got to the fair, Mike's son was upset. His favorite ride wasn't there.

**excited**

4. Mike was quiet until his son picked out a different ride.

**change**

5. Mike and his family played the same games they played last year.

**join**

6. Mike and his family helped a man take apart a puzzle and put it back together again.

# Word Game

**Write a word from the box under each clue. Then read the word made by the boxed letters. It tells what Martin Luther King, Jr., had for people in the United States.**

| join | upset | described | excited |
|------|-------|-----------|---------|
| calm | apart | change | |

**1.** told about what something was like

▢ __ __ __ __ __ __ __ __

**2.** away from each other

__ __ ▢ __ __

**3.** angry or not happy

__ __ ▢ __ __

**4.** to make different

__ __ ▢ __ __ __

**5.** sitting still and quiet

__ __ ▢ __

**6.** feeling very happy

__ __ __ __ __ __ __

**7.** to put together

__ __ __ __

# Standardized Test Practice

**Look for the word or words that have the same or almost the same meaning as the underlined word. Circle the letter beside your choice.**

**TIP**

Always read all the answer choices. Many choices may make sense. Only one answer choice has the same or almost the same meaning as the underlined word.

1. calm voice

   A quiet     C sad

   B happy     D angry

2. excited winner

   A sad     C new

   B angry     D happy

3. miles apart

   A not happy     C not old

   B not together     D not hot

4. upset child

   A young     C unhappy

   B glad     D smart

5. described the house

   A smiled about

   B told about

   C cleaned about

   D thought about

6. join your friends

   A come down

   B come together

   C come through

   D come away

7. tried to change

   A become sad

   B become bad

   C become different

   D become good

8. your dream

   A wish     C puddle

   B glass     D house

Vocabulary in Context



Vocabulary in Context G2, SV 9780547625751

# Related Words

Many people work for the government. These workers often have special titles. The words in the box are related because they name government jobs.

| officer | president | chairperson | mayor |

**Use the words in the box to finish the sentences.**

**1.** The leader of a city is a _______________.

**2.** A member of the police force is a police _______________.

**3.** The leader of a country is a _______________.

**4.** Someone in charge of a meeting is a _______________.

**Which job would you like to have? Draw a picture and write a sentence about why you would like the job.**



Word Skills

# Abbreviations

An abbreviation is a short form of a word. It usually begins with a capital letter and ends with a period. An abbreviation comes from letters in the word.

Ambassador Ying lives on Spencer Avenue.

Amb. Ying lives on Spencer Ave.

**Complete each person's name by writing an abbreviation. Use the underlined letters in the word in dark print. (Don't forget the capital letter and the period.)**

**president**  1. Our school is named after ________________ Lincoln.

**officer**  2. I see that ________________ Jake is in charge of traffic.

**captain**  3. The owner of the boat is ________________ Hakel.

**junior**  4. My dad's name is Robert Acosta. I am Robert Acosta, ________________.

**professor**  5. ________________ Wong teaches math at the college.

**Complete each place name by writing an abbreviation. Use the underlined letters in the word in dark print.**

**university**  6. My brother goes to the ________________ of Texas.

**saint**  7. My mom is a nurse at ________________ Mary's Hospital.

**route**  8. Turn left on ________________ 95.



Word Skills

# Expand Word Meaning

You don't have to work for the government to be an <u>ambassador</u>.

These sentences tell about another kind of <u>ambassador</u>.

Erin is an <u>ambassador</u> for the local animal shelter.

Jacob is an <u>ambassador</u> for healthy eating.

**What kind of <u>ambassador</u> would you like to be? Think about something important to you. Draw and write about yourself as an ambassador.**

**You can also be a <u>president</u>. What kind of club can you start? You can be president of your club. Draw and write about yourself as a president.**

**You can be a <u>chairperson</u>. What kind of meeting would you lead? Draw and write about yourself as a chairperson.**







Word Skills

# Writing

Martin Luther King, Jr., did not think it was fair that black and white children couldn't go to school together. He helped change that. Is there something you would like to change? How would you change it?

**On the lines below, write about something you would like to change someday. Use some vocabulary words from this unit in your writing.**

_______________________________________________

_______________________________________________

_______________________________________________

_______________________________________________

_______________________________________________

_______________________________________________

_______________________________________________

_______________________________________________

_______________________________________________



Writing

# The Magic of Masks

**Read the passage below. Think about the meanings of the words in dark print.**

---

In almost every African **village**, or small town, there is a **woodcarver**. This person makes wooden **masks** that can be scary, funny, or beautiful.

The masks are made to be worn. They are kept in a **hut**, or small house. On special days, people wear the masks. They also wear **costumes** that cover their bodies. Then they dance to the sound of drums.

In Africa, there are dances for many things. There is a dance when someone dies. There is a dance to make the **crops** grow. Some dances tell stories about how the world was made.

Most villages have a dance when girls or boys grow up. They use masks in these dances, too. The dances tell the boys and girls to act like **adults**. Then the whole village feels proud of its fine young men and women.

Dances with masks are an important part of life in Africa. Each village uses dances to teach people what is right and wrong. Children learn the **values** of their people from the masks made by the woodcarver.

**Go back to the passage. Underline the words or sentences that give you a clue to the meaning of each word in dark print.**

# Context Clues

**Read each sentence. Look for clues to help you finish each sentence with a word from the box. Write the word on the line.**

| | | | |
|---|---|---|---|
| woodcarver | masks | adults | crops |
| costumes | values | village | hut |



**1.** Every family has its own small house, or _______________________.

**2.** A _______________________ can make beautiful things out of wood.

**3.** The woodcarver made some scary _______________________.

**4.** Everyone who lives in the _______________________ knows everyone else.

**5.** Everyone in the village grows _______________________ for food.

**6.** People wear special _______________________ for the dance.

**7.** The _______________________ hope their children will learn from the dance.

**8.** Helping your family and your village are important African _______________________.

# Synonyms

**Synonyms are words that have the same or almost the same meaning. Draw a line under the word in the second sentence that matches the word or words in dark print in the first sentence.**

1. There are only ten families in my **small town**.
   I live in a village.

2. My father is **the person who makes wooden things** for the village.
   He is a woodcarver.

3. I stand in front of my **small house** to watch the dance.
   I come out of my hut to see it.

4. The children hope that they can dance when they are **grown-ups**.
   The people who are dancing are adults.

5. The adults wear **special clothes** for the dance.
   These costumes are worn for celebrations.

# Dictionary Skills

**Put the words in the box in ABC order. Write them on the lines.**

| woodcarver | masks | adults | crops |
|---|---|---|---|
| costumes | values | village | hut |

1. ___________________   5. ___________________

2. ___________________   6. ___________________

3. ___________________   7. ___________________

4. ___________________   8. ___________________





Unit 7
Vocabulary in Context G2, SV 9780547625751

# Word Puzzle

**Write a word from the box next to each clue. Then read the word made from the boxed letters. The letters in the boxes will spell the word in the last clue.**

| | | | |
|---|---|---|---|
| woodcarver | masks | adults | crops |
| costumes | values | village | hut |

**1.** I am a small town.

**2.** We look like faces, but we are made of wood or something else.

**3.** We are people who are grown up.

**4.** I am a small house.

**5.** I make things out of wood.

**6.** These are plants grown for food.

**7.** We are special clothes used for dances.

**8.** These are what you believe to be right and wrong.

# Standardized Test Practice

**Read each sentence. Pick the word that best completes the sentence. Circle the letter for the correct word.**

Read each sentence carefully. Use the other words in the sentences to help you choose each missing word.



1. A small town is a ____.

   **A** city      **C** country

   **B** village      **D** state

2. A person who makes things out of wood is a ____.

   **A** teacher      **C** mother

   **B** driver      **D** woodcarver

3. Faces made of wood are ____.

   **A** hats      **C** shirts

   **B** smiles      **D** masks

4. A small house is a ____.

   **A** car      **C** hut

   **B** boat      **D** castle

5. Plants grown for food are ____.

   **A** crops      **C** stars

   **B** hats      **D** pictures

6. Special clothes worn for celebrations are ____.

   **A** whistles      **C** costumes

   **B** horns      **D** pans

7. People who are grown up are ____.

   **A** children      **C** brothers

   **B** babies      **D** adults

8. The things you believe are right and wrong are your ____.

   **A** songs      **C** stories

   **B** values      **D** jokes

# Using Synonyms

These words are synonyms. They have similar meanings.

| fabulous   fantastic   marvelous   splendid   superb |

**Many costumes and masks look fantastic. What can you think of that looks fantastic? Draw or write to illustrate the meaning of the underlined words.**

| | |
|---|---|
| **1.** a <u>fantastic</u> TV show | **4.** a <u>fabulous</u> place to visit |
| **2.** a <u>marvelous</u> dinner | **5.** a <u>splendid</u> bicycle |
| **3.** a <u>superb</u> day | **6.** a <u>marvelous</u> birthday |

**Word Skills**

# Analogies

An analogy is a word puzzle. Think about how the first two words are related. Think of a word related to the third word in the same way.

bicycle–two is like tricycle–_______________________

A bicycle has two wheels. How many wheels does a tricycle have?

**Complete these word puzzles. Share your answers.**

1. fabulous–wonderful is like mad–_______________________

2. fifteen–number is like purple–_______________________

3. corn–vegetable is like banana–_______________________

4. quickly–quick is like slowly–_______________________

5. honey–sweet is like lemon–_______________________

6. yell–loud is like whisper–_______________________

7. hand–handprint is like foot–_______________________

8. water–cup is like food–_______________________

9. cotton–soft is like metal–_______________________

10. summer–hot is like winter–_______________________

11. horse–trot is like frog–_______________________

12. lumpy–smooth is like happy–_______________________

13. calf–cow is like cub–_______________________

14. France–country is like Texas–_______________________





Unit 7
Vocabulary in Context G2, SV 9780547625751

Word Skills

# Word Families

Words that have the same base word are part of the same <u>word family</u>.

whole + ly = wholly

**Add –<u>ly</u> to these words.**

**1.** fabulous + ly = _____________   **3.** marvelous + ly = _____________

**2.** splendid + ly = _____________   **4.** superb + ly = _____________

**Add –<u>ly</u> to these words. Then draw a picture to show the meaning of the new word.**

| | |
|---|---|
| **5.** glad + ly = _____________ | **7.** quick + ly = _____________ |
| **6.** sad + ly = _____________ | **8.** soft + ly = _____________ |

Word Skills

# Picture Cards

**Draw a picture of each word below.**

| | |
|---|---|
| **1. masks** | **5. fantastic** |
| **2. crops** | **6. woodcarver** |
| **3. costumes** | **7. adults** |
| **4. hut** | **8. splendid** |

Word Skills

Name _______________________________________________  Date _______________

# Writing

Imagine you are making a mask. How would it look?

**On the lines below, write about your mask. When would it be
worn? Who would wear it? What feelings would it show? Use some
vocabulary words from this unit in your writing.**

_______________________________________________

_______________________________________________

_______________________________________________

_______________________________________________

_______________________________________________

_______________________________________________

_______________________________________________

_______________________________________________

_______________________________________________

_______________________________________________



**77**
Unit 7
Vocabulary in Context G2, SV 9780547625751

# A Home in the Ground

**Read the passage below. Think about the meanings of the words in dark print.**

---

Did you know that ants are like people? They work together to get things done. Ants live in a large group called a **colony**. **Hundreds** of ants live in each colony. Each ant has its own job. Together the ants help their colony grow. Most ant colonies are in the ground. A colony has many cozy little rooms.

Most ants in a colony are worker ants. They find food, care for the baby ants, and make the colony bigger. Worker ants are very strong. If a worker ant finds food that is too big to carry, other worker ants help. But a **single** worker ant can carry something 50 times its own **weight**. That would be the same as a person being able to **lift** an elephant!

The worker ants also care for the **queen** ant. Her job is to lay eggs. This is the only thing she does. There may be one or more queens in each colony. They live for 5 to 15 **years**. During that time, each queen lays **thousands** of eggs. These eggs become baby ants. This makes much work for the worker ants. It's no wonder that ants are everywhere!

**Go back to the passage. Underline the words or sentences that give you a clue to the meaning of each word in dark print.**

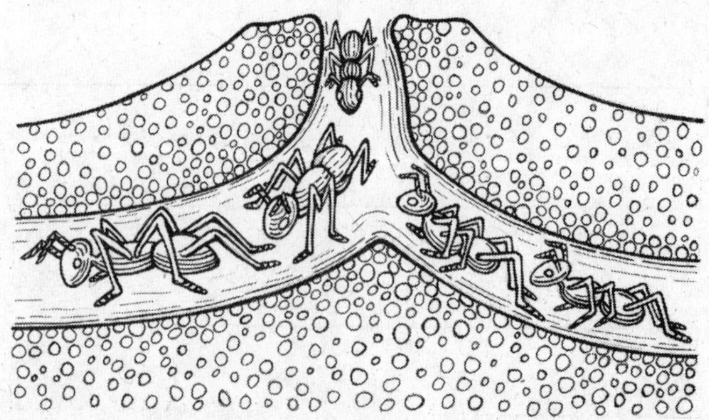

# Context Clues

**Meanings for the vocabulary words are given below. Go back to the passage and read each sentence that has a vocabulary word. If you still cannot tell the meaning, look for clues in the sentences that come before and after the one with the vocabulary word. Write each word from the box in front of its meaning.**

| | | | |
|---|---|---|---|
| colony | lift | thousands | queen |
| weight | single | hundreds | years |

1. _____________________ : to pick up

2. _____________________ : more than 12 months

3. _____________________ : how heavy something is

4. _____________________ : an ant that lays eggs

5. _____________________ : more than 1,000

6. _____________________ : a group of ants living together

7. _____________________ : more than 100

8. _____________________ : only one

Vocabulary in Context

# Classifying

**Study each group of words. Think about how they are alike. Then finish each group with a word or words from the box. Add another word that you know to each group.**

| thousands   colony   queen   hundreds   years |
|---|



## 1. Numbers
tens

_______________________

_______________________

_______________________

## 2. Time
days

_______________________

_______________________

## 3. Rulers
king

_______________________

_______________________

## 4. Places to Live
house

lodge

_______________________

_______________________

# Crossword Puzzle

**Use the clues and the words in the box to finish the crossword puzzle.**

Vocabulary in Context

**Across**

**2.** how heavy something is

**4.** more than 100

**6.** an ant that lays eggs

**7.** only one

**8.** more than 12 months

**Down**

**1.** to pick up

**3.** more than 1,000

**5.** group of ants





Vocabulary in Context G2, SV 9780547625751

# Standardized Test Practice

**Read each sentence. Pick the word that best completes the sentence.
Circle the letter for the correct word.**

**TIP**

Use each answer choice in place of the underlined word or
words. Remember that the underlined word or words and your
answer must have the same or almost the same meaning.

1. Only one is ____.

   A single        C two

   B small         D five

2. How heavy something is is
   its ____.

   A head          C weight

   B arm           D age

3. To pick up is to ____.

   A lift          C count

   B talk          D think

4. Something that lasts more
   than 12 months lasts ____.

   A days          C weeks

   B tens          D years

5. An ant that lays eggs is
   a ____.

   A parent        C child

   B queen         D teacher

6. A group of ants is a ____.

   A house         C colony

   B bird          D person

7. More than 100 is ____.

   A hundreds      C tens

   B fives         D twos

8. More than 1,000 is ____.

   A tens          C thousands

   B threes        D fours





Vocabulary in Context

# Content-Area Words

The following words have special meanings in science. The words are used to tell about all living things, including ants.

| category    family    similar    species    specimen |
| --- |

**This chart shows how scientists use these words. What animal is the chart about? Fill in the last box.**

| | |
| --- | --- |
| KINGDOM | **Animal** |
| CLASS | **Mammal** (warmblooded, has hair or fur) |
| ORDER | **Carnivore** (eats meat) |
| FAMILY | **Cat** (includes cats of all sizes) |
| SPECIES | ____ ____ ____ ____ (has stripes) |

Each category in the chart tells about the tiger.
The tiger is similar to other animals in many ways.
The cat family is very large. The tiger is one species of cat.
To see a specimen, you have to visit a zoo. A specimen is "one."

**What other species do you think belong to the cat family?**
**Draw and label a specimen. How is your cat similar to a tiger?**

Word Skills



Vocabulary in Context G2, SV 9780547625751

# Multiple-Meaning Words

Some words have special scientific meanings, but they also have everyday meanings.

> My kitten Jingles is a member of the cat <u>family</u>.
> Jingles is also a member of my <u>family</u>!

**Complete the sentences. Share your ideas with classmates.**

1. My friend and I have <u>similar</u> ______________________.

2. That ______________________ is a sad <u>specimen</u>!

3. Apples, bananas, and oranges belong in the ______________________ <u>category</u>.

4. The ______________________ is so good that it must be a special <u>species</u>!

**Draw and label pictures for two of the sentences above.**

<table>
<tr><td><br><br><br><br><br><br><br><br></td><td></td></tr>
</table>







Word Skills

# Analogies

Look at the following word puzzles. Think about how the first two words go together. What one word completes each puzzle?

roar–tiger                  dog–puppy                  birds–bird

meow–____________        bear–____________        ants–____________

**Complete these word puzzles. Remember to think about how the first two words go together.**

| | |
|---|---|
| **1.** moon–night <br><br> sun–________________ | **6.** mittens–hands <br><br> boots–________________ |
| **2.** man–king <br><br> woman–________________ | **7.** doctor–Dr. <br><br> street–________________ |
| **3.** mouse–mice <br><br> tooth–________________ | **8.** hard–soft <br><br> rough–________________ |
| **4.** nose–smell <br><br> eyes–________________ | **9.** fish–scales <br><br> bird–________________ |
| **5.** learn–classroom <br><br> sleep–________________ | **10.** sock–foot <br><br> glove–________________ |

Word Skills

# Using Context

**Use the context clues to help you understand the meaning of the underlined words. Answer the questions by drawing or writing.**

**1.** The twins look so <u>similar</u> it is hard to tell them apart. What two things can you think of that are <u>similar</u>?

**3.** A <u>family</u> of ants works together in a colony. How does your <u>family</u> work together?

**2.** There are many <u>species</u> of insects. What animal <u>species</u> is your favorite?

**4.** You can group tissue paper and notecards in the paper <u>category</u>. What kinds of things can be grouped in the metal <u>category</u>?

Word Skills


 Vocabulary in Context G2, SV 9780547625751

# Writing

Ants are very tiny. What do you think it would be like to be as small as an ant? What does their home look like? How do they feel? What do they do?

**Write a story about ants on the lines below. Use some vocabulary words from this unit in your writing.**

_______________________________________________

_______________________________________________

_______________________________________________

_______________________________________________

_______________________________________________

_______________________________________________

_______________________________________________

_______________________________________________

_______________________________________________



Vocabulary in Context G2, SV 9780547625751

# Animals on the Farm

**Read the passage below. Think about the meanings of the words in dark print.**

The red rooster crows loudly. The **farmer** smiles as he eats his eggs and ham and drinks his milk. This food came from the animals he cares for when he does his **chores** each day.

There is a large **herd** of cattle eating grass in the **pasture**. Many of the cattle are dark red. They will go to **market** and be sold for meat. The other cattle are black and white. The farmer gets milk from these cattle.

The pigs are sleeping in their pen. They are quite fat. They will be ready for market soon. The farmer gets meat from the pigs.

The farmer must **raise** sheep where crops won't grow. You can often see a **flock** of many sheep **grazing** on a hill. The farmer gets meat and wool from the sheep. Their soft wool is used to make rugs and clothes.

The hens are eating corn on the ground. The rooster watches over the hens. The hens lay eggs. The eggs are white, brown, or spotted. Many of the eggs are sold at the market.

The farmer works hard to care for his animals. But they give him much in return!

**Go back to the passage. Underline the words or sentences that give you a clue to the meaning of each word in dark print.**

# Context Clues

**Meanings for the vocabulary words are given below. Go back to the passage and read each sentence that has a vocabulary word. If you still cannot tell the meaning, look for clues in the sentences that come before and after the one with the vocabulary word. Write each word from the box in front of its meaning.**

| | | | |
|---|---|---|---|
| farmer | chores | herd | pasture |
| market | raise | flock | grazing |

1. _________________: a group of sheep or birds

2. _________________: work that must be done each day

3. _________________: grassy land that animals use for food

4. _________________: a person who works on a farm

5. _________________: a group of large animals

6. _________________: to help something grow

7. _________________: eating grass

8. _________________: a place where farmers sell animals and other things







Unit 9
Vocabulary in Context G2, SV 9780547625751

# Understanding Multiple-Meaning Words

**The words in the boxes have more than one meaning. Look for clues in each sentence to tell which meaning is used. Write the letter of the meaning next to the correct sentence.**

| herd | **a.** a group of large animals |
| | **b.** to join together |

1. ________________: The farmer will <u>herd</u> the animals into the barn.

2. ________________: One of the farmer's chores is to feed the <u>herd</u> of cattle.

| raise | **a.** to lift up |
| | **b.** to help to grow |

3. ________________: I <u>raise</u> the flag every morning.

4. ________________: My aunt and uncle <u>raise</u> pigs and chickens.

| flock | **a.** a group of sheep or birds |
| | **b.** to go in a group |

5. ________________: I saw a <u>flock</u> of ducks yesterday.

6. ________________: People <u>flock</u> to the market.

| grazing | **a.** lightly touching |
| | **b.** eating grass |

7. ________________: The cattle are <u>grazing</u> in the pasture.

8. ________________: Her sleeve was <u>grazing</u> the top of the desk.

# Word Map

**Words can be put on a kind of map to show that they are alike.
Write each word from the box in the group where it belongs to tell
about farm animals. Then add a word you know to each group.**

| herd | flock | pasture |
|---|---|---|
| raise | chores | grazing |

**How They Eat**

chewing

_____________________

_____________________

_____________________

**Where They Go**

barn

_____________________

_____________________

_____________________

**FARM ANIMALS**

**Work Done for Them**

feeding

_____________________

_____________________

_____________________

**Groups of Them**

family

_____________________

_____________________

_____________________

Name _________________________________________ Date ________________________

# Standardized Test Practice

**Read each sentence. Pick the word that best completes the sentence.
Circle the letter for the correct word.**

**TIP**

Read each sentence carefully. Use the other words in
the sentences to help you choose each missing word.



**1.** A group of sheep or birds is a
____.

A flock      C family

B class      D school

**2.** Grassy land that animals use
for food is a ____.

A room      C house

B pasture    D yard

**3.** A place where farmers sell
animals is a ____.

A field      C store

B pasture    D market

**4.** Work that must be done each
day is called ____.

A play       C chores

B sleep      D read

**5.** A person who works on a farm
is called a ____.

A teacher    C nurse

B farmer     D doctor

**6.** When people help something
grow, they ____ it.

A see        C taste

B raise      D run

**7.** A group of large animals is a
____.

A map        C herd

B mark       D mask

**8.** When animals are eating
grass, they are ____.

A grazing    C playing

B helping    D sleeping



Vocabulary in Context G2, SV 9780547625751

## Related Words

The words in the box are related. Some name animals. Some name people. Some name both.

| beasts    beings    creatures    critters    vermin |

**Draw pictures to illustrate the labels.**

| human <u>beings</u> | furry <u>creatures</u> |
|---|---|
| pesty <u>vermin</u> | farm <u>beasts</u> |
| cute <u>critters</u> | my favorite <u>creatures</u> |

Word Skills

# Expand Word Meaning

We can use one word in many different ways. Beasts are animals, but sometimes we say that people act more like beasts than animals do!

Cows and horses are helpful <u>beasts</u>.
I think that rude people are <u>beastly</u>.

**Add to each category. Write words. Draw pictures. Be a creative creature!**

| Make-Believe Critters | Creature Comforts |
|---|---|
| dragons | tasty food |
| **Ways to Act Beastly** | **Things to Say to Vermin** |
| yelling in class | shoo |

Word Skills



Vocabulary in Context G2, SV 9780547625751

# Regionalisms

People who live in different places often use different words to name the same thing. The underlined words have the same meaning. Which word do you usually say?

Horses are nice <u>animals</u>.
Horses are nice <u>critters</u>.
Horses are nice <u>beasts</u>.

**Circle the word or words you use. Draw a picture.**

| | |
|---|---|
| porch   lanai<br><br>patio   stoop | frying pan   spider<br><br>skillet |
| pancakes   hot cakes<br><br>flapjacks | paper bag   sack<br><br>tote   poke |





Word Skills

Unit 9
Vocabulary in Context G2, SV 9780547625751

## Draw and Label

Draw a picture of a farm below. Then use the words in the box to label things you drew in your picture. Use as many words as you can.

| | | | | |
|---|---|---|---|---|
| beasts | farmer | chores | creatures | herd |
| pasture | beings | market | critters | raise |
| flock | grazing | vermin | | |

# Writing

Think about an animal you or someone you know has cared for. What kind of animal is it? What color is it? What are some of the best things about it? Tell how to take care of the animal each day.

**On the lines below, write about an animal that you or someone you know has cared for. Use some vocabulary words from this unit in your writing.**

_______________________________________________________

_______________________________________________________

_______________________________________________________

_______________________________________________________

_______________________________________________________

_______________________________________________________

_______________________________________________________

_______________________________________________________

_______________________________________________________

_______________________________________________________

# Nellie Bly

**Read the passage below. Think about the meanings of the words in dark print.**

---

In 1878, few women had jobs. They took care of their children and their homes. Elizabeth Cochrane wanted to be a writer. So she became a **reporter** when she grew up. She used the name Nellie Bly when she wrote.

Nellie Bly cared about poor people. She went into part of a city where the poorest people lived. She saw many people **crowded** together in old, broken-down buildings. The buildings weren't **safe** to live in. Still, the people who owned them would not **repair**, or fix, them. Nellie wrote an **article** to tell about the buildings. She put her story in the **newspaper** so everyone could read it.

Then Nellie went to see where many of the poor people worked. She found that children had to work there, too. These places were not safe. Many bosses were not **fair** to their workers. Nellie wrote an article about this.

Soon, **laws** were passed to make the lives of the poor people better. Nellie Bly was happy. She helped many people. She led the way for many women to become reporters!

**Go back to the passage. Underline the words or sentences that give you a clue to the meaning of each word in dark print.**

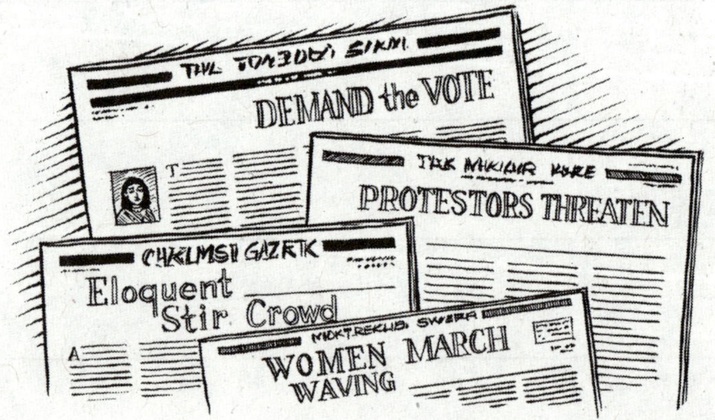




Vocabulary in Context G2, SV 9780547625751

# Context Clues

**Meanings for the vocabulary words are given below. Go back to
the passage and read each sentence that has a vocabulary word.
If you still cannot tell the meaning, look for clues in the sentences
that come before and after the one with the vocabulary word. Write
each word from the box in front of its meaning.**

| | | | |
|---|---|---|---|
| crowded | reporter | repair | laws |
| newspaper | article | safe | fair |

1. _________________: sheets of paper that tell about what just happened

2. _________________: too close to each other

3. _________________: to fix

4. _________________: rules made for all people

5. _________________: person who writes for a newspaper

6. _________________: free from danger

7. _________________: right

8. _________________: a story for a newspaper

# Cloze Paragraph

**Use words in the box to finish the paragraph. Read the paragraph again to be sure it makes sense.**

| | | | |
|---|---|---|---|
| crowded | reporter | repair | laws |
| newspaper | article | safe | fair |



A _________________ is a person who writes stories. These stories
(1)

are put in a _________________ so people can read them. Many
(2)

stories are _________________ on every page. A reporter can tell
(3)

people if a building is not _________________. Then the people who
(4)

own it will have to _________________ it. A reporter can find out if
(5)

something is right, or _________________. If it is not, the reporter can
(6)

write a(n) _________________ about it. This can help make sure that
(7)

_________________ are passed to keep it from happening anymore.
(8)

# Word Riddles

**Read each riddle. Use words from the box to answer each riddle.**

| | | | |
|---|---|---|---|
| crowded | reporter | repair | laws |
| newspaper | article | safe | fair |

**1.** I can fix things.

What can I do? ___________________

**2.** I have stories that tell about what just happened.

What am I? ___________________

**3.** We are too close together.

What are we? ___________________

**4.** I am free from danger.

What am I? ___________________

**5.** I am someone who writes for a newspaper.

Who am I? ___________________

**6.** I am a story in a newspaper.

What am I? ___________________

**7.** I do what is right.

What am I? ___________________

**8.** We are rules for all people.

What are we? ___________________







Vocabulary in Context

# Standardized Test Practice

**Read each sentence. Pick the word that best completes the sentence.**
**Circle the letter for the correct word.**

**TIP**
Read carefully. Use the other words in the sentences to help you choose each missing word.



**1.** The _____ won a prize for her story.

**A** runner      **C** reporter

**B** nurse      **D** firefighter

**2.** Did you see my picture in the _____?

**A** flower      **C** letter

**B** cloud      **D** newspaper

**3.** The people were _____ together in the small room.

**A** crowded      **C** written

**B** jumped      **D** swam

**4.** It isn't _____ to play with fire.

**A** happy      **C** wrong

**B** quiet      **D** safe

**5.** Megan's dad will _____ her broken bicycle.

**A** tear      **C** fight

**B** repair      **D** ride

**6.** I saw an _____ in the newspaper about schools.

**A** orange      **C** egg

**B** article      **D** ant

**7.** It is not _____ to lie to others.

**A** fair      **C** mean

**B** warm      **D** thick

**8.** _____ help us live together happily.

**A** Jugs      **C** Laws

**B** Bats      **D** Cars

# Using Context

These words all mean "to do something again."

| recount   recycle   rethink   retrace   review |
| --- |

**Read the sentences. Use context clues to figure out the meanings of the underlined words. Write or draw pictures to explain the meanings.**

| | |
| --- | --- |
| **1.** We are lost. We have to <u>retrace</u> our steps. | **4.** I'm saving these old newspapers. They can be <u>recycled</u>. |
| **2.** I should have ten pens, not nine pens. I will <u>recount</u> the pens. | **5.** This plan will not work. We have to <u>rethink</u> our ideas. |
| **3.** We're having a spelling test. Let's <u>review</u> our spelling words. | **6.** You counted 20, but I counted 22. We have to do a <u>recount</u>. |

**Word Skills**



Vocabulary in Context G2, SV 9780547625751

# Prefixes

These words start with the same prefix.

<u>re</u>think means "to think again"    <u>re</u>count means "to count again"
<u>re</u>trace means "to trace again"    <u>re</u>view means "to view again"

**Add <u>re</u>- to each word. Write words or draw a picture to explain the meaning of the new word.**

| | |
|---|---|
| **1.** use _______________ | **5.** turn _______________ |
| **2.** write _______________ | **6.** unite _______________ |
| **3.** paint _______________ | **7.** read _______________ |
| **4.** heat _______________ | **8.** play _______________ |

# Content-Area Words

When things are recycled, they are reused.

Old newspapers can be <u>recycled</u> to make new paper.
A broken table can be <u>recycled</u> by repairing it.

**Brainstorm ideas for each category. Write or draw pictures to express your ideas. Share your ideas with classmates.**

| THINGS THAT CAN BE RECYCLED | WAYS TO RECYCLE THINGS |
|---|---|
|  |  |

Word Skills

# Focus on Context

**Use the context clues to choose the correct answers. Circle your answer choice.**

1. We don't need our old magazines, so we will (recycle, recount) them.

2. I can't remember where I put my slippers, so I'll (review, retrace) my steps.

3. Let's (recount, review) our addition facts before the quiz.

4. I'm not sure that I have enough money, so I'll (recount, rethink) my coins.

5. We will need to (rethink, recycle) our plans if our soccer game is rained out.

**Choose one of the sentences above and draw a picture of its meaning.**



Vocabulary in Context G2, SV 9780547625751

Word Skills

Name _______________________________ Date _______________________________

# Writing

A newspaper reporter is always looking for a good story to write about. A good reporter watches everything that happens around him or her. Then the reporter writes stories about these things.

**Imagine you are a newspaper reporter. Tell about something that has just happened. Be sure to tell how, when, why, and where it happened. Use some vocabulary words from this unit in your writing.**

**The Times**

_______________________________

(date)


     Vocabulary in Context G2, SV 9780547625751

# Glossary

**A**

| | | |
|---|---|---|
| **adults** | *noun* | people who are grown up (page 68) |
| **airport** | *noun* | place where airplanes land and take off (page 23) |
| **amazing** | *adjective* | very surprising and wonderful (page 28) |
| **ambassador** | *noun* | a person sent to another country to represent his or her government (page 65) |
| **apart** | *adverb* | not together (page 59) |
| **apartment** | *noun* | a building with groups of rooms to live in (page 35) |
| **article** | *noun* | a story written for a newspaper (page 98) |
| **astronaut** | *noun* | a person who flies into space (page 38) |

**B**

| | | |
|---|---|---|
| **banquet** | *noun* | a big dinner for many people (page 49) |
| **beasts** | *noun* | large or wild animals (page 93) |
| **beavers** | *noun* | animals with soft fur, flat tails, and large front teeth (page 28) |
| **beings** | *noun* | living things (page 93) |
| **bellow** | *noun* | a deep, roaring sound (page 12) |
| **blast** | *verb* | to blow apart with a loud noise (page 44) |
| **blocks** | *verb* | stops something from passing by (page 28) |
| **branches** | *noun* | the parts of a tree growing out from its trunk (page 8) |
| **burrows** | *noun* | homes dug in the ground by animals (page 33) |

**C**

| | | |
|---|---|---|
| **cabin** | *noun* | a small house often made of logs (page 35) |
| **calm** | *adjective* | quiet and still (page 59) |



Vocabulary in Context G2; SV 9780547625751

| **carpenters** | *noun* | people who build and repair wooden buildings (page 28) |
| **castle** | *noun* | a large stone building or group of buildings with thick walls, towers, and other defenses against attack (page 36) |
| **category** | *noun* | group (page 83) |
| **cave** | *noun* | an opening in the side of a hill (page 33) |
| **celebrating** | *verb* | honoring a special day or time (page 49) |
| **center** | *noun* | middle (page 44) |
| **chairperson** | *noun* | a person who leads a meeting (page 64) |
| **change** | *verb* | to become different (page 58) |
| **chores** | *noun* | work that must be done each day (page 88) |
| **circular** | *adjective* | having the form of a circle (page 43) |
| **cloud** | *noun* | a white or gray mass of water vapor floating high in the sky (page 44) |
| **coil** | *verb* | to roll and twist (page 53) |
| **colony** | *noun* | a group of ants living together (page 78) |
| **countryside** | *noun* | an open area of country (page 23) |
| **costumes** | *noun* | special clothes worn for celebrations (page 68) |
| **cottage** | *noun* | a small country house (page 35) |
| **cozy** | *adjective* | warm and dry (page 28) |
| **creatures** | *noun* | animals (page 93) |
| **critters** | *noun* | animals (page 93) |
| **croak** | *noun* | a low, hoarse sound (page 12) |
| **crops** | *noun* | plants that are grown for food (page 68) |
| **crowded** | *adjective* | too close to each other (page 98) |



Vocabulary in Context G2, SV 9780547625751

# D

**dam**   *noun*   a wall built to hold back water (page 28)

**danger**   *noun*   a chance of being hurt (page 8)

**decorations**   *noun*   things used to make a place look special (page 48)

**described**   *verb*   told about or wrote about (page 59)

**desk**   *noun*   furniture with a top for use in writing or reading (page 23)

**diet**   *noun*   foods a person eats every day (page 18)

**dream**   *noun*   a wish (page 59)

# E

**enemies**   *noun*   people or a group who try to hurt someone else (page 28)

**energy**   *noun*   the power to work (page 18)

**envelopes**   *noun*   wrappers made of paper, used for mailing (page 49)

**excited**   *adjective*   very happy (page 58)

**exercise**   *noun*   the moving of the body in work or play (page 18)

**experiments**   *noun*   tests that help people find out about things (page 38)

# F

**fabulous**   *adjective*   wonderful; exciting (page 73)

**fair**   *adjective*   right (page 98)

**family**   *noun*   a group of living things that are related (page 83)

**fantastic**   *adjective*   causing wonder or surprise (page 73)

**farmer**   *noun*   a person who works on a farm (page 88)

| **farmland** | *noun* | land used for farming (page 23) |
| **field** | *noun* | open area of land (page 23) |
| **firecrackers** | *noun* | paper tubes that make loud noises when you light them (page 49) |
| **flight** | *noun* | the act of flying (page 38) |
| **flock** | *noun* | a group of sheep or birds (page 88) |
| **form** | *verb* | to make (page 8) |
| **frighten** | *verb* | to make afraid (page 48) |
| **fruit** | *noun* | a food that tastes sweet and grows on trees or bushes (page 8) |

## G

| **gardener** | *noun* | someone who gardens (page 25) |
| **grain** | *noun* | the seed of wheat, oats, corn, and other cereal grasses (page 18) |
| **grazing** | *verb* | eating grass (page 88) |
| **gym** | *noun* | a room or building with equipment to exercise (page 23) |

## H

| **harvest** | *noun* | the picking of crops (page 18) |
| **healthy** | *adjective* | not sick; good for the body (page 18) |
| **herd** | *noun* | a group of large animals (page 88) |
| **hoot** | *noun* | a kind of cry (page 12) |
| **hundreds** | *noun* | groups of 100 (page 78) |
| **hut** | *noun* | a small house (page 68) |

## J

| **join** | *verb* | to come into or come together with (page 59) |





**Glossary**
Vocabulary in Context G2, SV 9780547625751

# L

**lair**  *noun*  a den or resting place of a wild animal (page 33)

**laws**  *noun*  rules made by a country or state for all the people who live there (page 98)

**levels**  *noun*  various heights that are tall or short (page 8)

**lift**  *verb*  to pick up (page 78)

**lodge**  *noun*  a home of sticks and mud built in a pond by beavers; a cabin or a small shelter (pages 28, 34)

# M

**market**  *noun*  a place where farmers sell animals and other things (page 88)

**marvelous**  *adjective*  wonderful (page 73)

**masks**  *noun*  faces made of wood or other things to be worn on special days (page 68)

**mayor**  *noun*  the leader of a city (page 64)

**meadow**  *noun*  land that is mostly covered with grass (page 23)

# N

**newspaper**  *noun*  sheets of paper that tell about what happened (page 98)

# O

**officer**  *noun*  a member of a police force (page 64)

**orbit**  *noun*  a path that curves completely around something (page 43)



Vocabulary in Context G2, SV 9780547625751

# P

| | | |
|---|---|---|
| **pasture** | *noun* | grassy land that animals use for food (pages 23, 88) |
| **planets** | *noun* | bodies in space that move around the sun (page 38) |
| **pollution** | *noun* | something that people do that hurts the earth (page 8) |
| **pounced** | *verb* | jumped on something suddenly and took hold (page 49) |
| **pranced** | *verb* | walked and danced (page 49) |
| **president** | *noun* | the leader of a country (page 64) |

# Q

| | | |
|---|---|---|
| **queen** | *noun* | an ant that lays eggs (page 78) |

# R

| | | |
|---|---|---|
| **rain forest** | *noun* | a very thick forest in a place where it is wet all year (page 8) |
| **raise** | *verb* | to help something grow (page 88) |
| **ranch** | *noun* | a large farm for raising herds of animals (page 36) |
| **ranch** | *verb* | to work on a ranch (page 36) |
| **recount** | *verb* | to count again (page 103) |
| **recycle** | *verb* | to use again (page 103) |
| **repair** | *verb* | to fix (page 98) |
| **reporter** | *noun* | a person who writes for a newspaper (page 98) |
| **rest** | *noun* | a state of sleeping (page 18) |
| **rethink** | *verb* | to think again (page 103) |
| **retrace** | *verb* | to trace again (page 103) |

| **review** | *verb* | to view or study again (page 103) |
| **revolving** | *verb* | turning around on a center point (page 43) |
| **roost** | *noun* | a place birds use for sitting and resting (page 33) |

## S

| **safe** | *adjective* | free from danger (page 98) |
| **satellites** | *noun* | machines in space that send pictures back to Earth (page 38) |
| **shuttle** | *noun* | a spaceship with wings that can be used many times (page 38) |
| **similar** | *noun* | alike (page 83) |
| **single** | *adjective* | only one (page 78) |
| **sizes** | *noun* | how big things are (page 8) |
| **species** | *noun* | type (page 83) |
| **specimen** | *noun* | one of something (page 83) |
| **spinning** | *verb* | twisting and turning in a circle (page 43) |
| **spiral** | *noun* | a circling line that curves around a center point (page 43) |
| **splendid** | *adjective* | very good (page 73) |
| **star** | *noun* | an object in the sky at night that shines by its own light (page 44) |
| **studied** | *verb* | tried to learn about something (page 38) |
| **superb** | *adjective* | very fine; excellent (page 73) |
| **swirl** | *verb* | to spin and twist (page 53) |

## T

| **thousands** | *noun* | groups of 1,000 (page 78) |
| **tractor** | *noun* | a machine used on a farm (page 18) |
| **training** | *noun* | teaching (page 38) |

| **twirl** | *verb* | to spin and twist (page 53) |
| **twist** | *verb* | to turn with a winding movement (page 53) |

## U

| **upset** | *adjective* | unhappy (page 59) |

## V

| **values** | *noun* | things a person believes to be right and wrong (page 68) |
| **vermin** | *noun* | small, harmful animals or insects (page 93) |
| **village** | *noun* | a small town (page 68) |

## W

| **warble** | *noun* | a song-like sound (page 12) |
| **weight** | *noun* | how heavy something is (page 78) |
| **whirl** | *verb* | to spin (page 53) |
| **woodcarver** | *noun* | a person who makes things from wood (page 68) |

## Y

| **years** | *noun* | groups of 12 months (page 78) |
| **yowl** | *noun* | a kind of whine (page 12) |



Vocabulary in Context G2, SV 9780547625751

# Answer Key

## Page 9

1. rain forest
2. sizes
3. levels
4. branches
5. fruit
6. form
7. pollution
8. danger

## Page 10

1. branches
2. danger
3. fruit
4. levels
5. pollution

Additional words will vary.

## Page 11

1. B
2. C
3. A
4. C
5. D
6. A
7. C
8. B

## Page 12

Drawings will vary based on students' personal experiences.

## Page 13

1. bellow; yowl
2. bellow; croak; hoot; warble
3. Accept all reasonable answers.
4. Accept all reasonable answers.
5. croak
6. warble

Additional words will vary.

## Page 14

Possible answers are given. Accept reasonable answers.

1. shouted
2. asked
3. squealed
4. sighed
5. screamed
6. growled

## Page 15

Word search puzzles will vary but should include all vocabulary words.

## Page 16

Drawings and labels will vary but should include as many vocabulary words as possible.




**116**

**Answer Key**
Vocabulary in Context G2, SV 9780547625751

## Page 17
Answers will vary based on students' personal experiences.

## Page 19
1. grain

2. tractor

3. diet

4. harvest

5. healthy

6. rest

7. energy

8. exercise

## Page 20
**Dictionary Skills**
1. farm machine

2. picking of crops

3. food

4. work

5. sleep

6. power

7. wheat, oats, corn

8. not sick

**Relating Words**
1. Possible answer: Farmers can drive tractors to the fields.

2. Possible answer: Farmers pick their crops and sell them at the market.

## Page 21
**Across**
1. diet

3. harvest

5. grain

7. exercise

**Down**
2. tractor

4. energy

6. healthy

8. rest

## Page 22
1. D

2. C

3. B

4. C

5. A

6. D

7. A

8. D

## Page 23
field; pasture; farmland; meadow; countryside

Additional words will vary but should relate to farms.

## Page 24
1. inside; outside; sidewalk

2. grassland; dreamland; landmark

3. cornfield; hayfield; fieldwork




**117**

**Answer Key**
Vocabulary in Context G2, SV 9780547625751

4. backyard; farmyard; yardstick

5. henhouse; farmhouse;
   houseboat/boathouse

6. Drawings will vary but should illustrate one
   compound word in the activity.

## Page 25

1. small

2. cow

3. sand

4. sad

5. gardener

6. bird

## Page 26
**Adding -ed and -ing**

Paragraphs should relate to farming and
include one of the forms of pick.

## Picture Cards

Drawings will vary but should demonstrate an
understanding of the words.

## Page 27

Answers will vary based on students' personal
experiences.

## Page 29

1. carpenters

2. Beavers

3. lodge

4. cozy

5. enemies

6. amazing

7. blocks

8. dam

## Page 30

1. carpenters

2. beavers

3. amazing

4. lodge

5. cozy

6. enemies

7. blocks

8. dam

## Page 31
**Word Groups**

1. dam

2. beavers

3. carpenters

4. cozy

5. amazing

6. blocks

7. lodge

8. enemies

## Dictionary Skills

1. build, carpenter, home, tools

2. dry, lodge, mud, water

## Page 32

1. A

2. B

3. A

4. C

5. C

6. D

7. A

8. B

**Page 33**

1. B

2. B

3. A

4. A

**Page 34**

Drawings will vary but should demonstrate an understanding of the underlined words.

**Page 35**

1. lair; lodge; burrow; cave; roost

2. Answers will vary.

3. cottage; apartment; house; cabin; tent

4. Answers will vary.

**Page 36**
**Riddles**

1. cabin

2. house

3. cave

4. castle

5. ranch

**Words with -ed and -ing**
Sentences will vary.

**Page 37**
Answers will vary based on students' personal experiences.

**Page 39**
**Context Clues**

1. astronaut

2. training

3. experiments

4. satellites

5. studied

6. planets

**Class Survey**
Questions and tally marks will vary.

**Page 40**

1. astronaut

2. flight

3. planets

4. shuttle

5. studied

6. training

7. experiments

8. satellites

**Page 41**

1. planets

2. astronaut

**3.** shuttle

**4.** experiments

**Page 42**

1. D

2. C

3. D

4. B

5. C

6. A

7. B

8. A

**Page 43**

Drawings will vary but should demonstrate an understanding of the underlined words.

**Page 44**

Answers will vary but should belong to the word families.

**Page 45**

1. A

2. B

3. A

4. C

5. C

6. B

**Page 46**

Drawings and labels will vary but should include as many vocabulary words as possible.

**Page 47**

Answers will vary based on students' personal experiences.

**Page 50**
**Context Clues**

1. decorations

2. envelopes

3. pranced

4. frighten

5. banquet

6. firecrackers

7. pounced

8. celebrating

**Riddles**

1. envelopes

2. decorations

3. frighten

**Page 51**

1. banquet

2. firecrackers

3. pounced

4. decorations

Additional words will vary.

**Page 52**

1. C

2. D

3. B

4. C



Vocabulary in Context G2, SV 9780547625751

**5.** A

**6.** A

**7.** B

**8.** D

## Page 53

Drawings will vary but should relate to vocabulary words.

## Page 54

**1.** spin

**2.** twist

**3.** turn

**4.** twirl; whirl; swirl

**5.** coil

**6.** ring

Additional words will vary but should rhyme.

## Page 55

Drawings will vary but should demonstrate an understanding of the blended words.

## Page 56

Word search puzzles will vary but should include all vocabulary words.

## Page 57

Answers will vary based on students' personal experiences.

## Page 60

**1.** upset

**2.** described

**3.** apart

**4.** excited

**5.** dream

**6.** join

**7.** change

**8.** calm

## Page 61

**1.** happy

**2.** together

**3.** upset

**4.** quiet

**5.** same

**6.** take apart

## Page 62

**1.** described

**2.** apart

**3.** upset

**4.** change

**5.** calm

**6.** excited

**7.** join

Answer to puzzle: dream

## Page 63

**1.** A

**2.** D

**3.** B

**4.** C

**5.** B



Vocabulary in Context G2, SV 9780547625751

**6.** B

**7.** C

**8.** A

## Page 64

**1.** mayor

**2.** officer

**3.** president

**4.** chairperson

Pictures and sentences will vary.

## Page 65

**1.** Pres.

**2.** Off.

**3.** Capt.

**4.** Jr.

**5.** Prof.

**6.** Univ.

**7.** St.

**8.** Rte.

## Page 66

Drawings and answers will vary.

## Page 67

Answers will vary based on students' personal experiences.

## Page 69

**1.** hut

**2.** woodcarver

**3.** masks

**4.** village

**5.** crops

**6.** costumes

**7.** adults

**8.** values

## Page 70
### Synonyms

**1.** village

**2.** woodcarver

**3.** hut

**4.** adults

**5.** costumes

### Dictionary Skills

**1.** adults

**2.** costumes

**3.** crops

**4.** hut

**5.** masks

**6.** values

**7.** village

**8.** woodcarver

## Page 71

**1.** village

**2.** masks

**3.** adults

**4.** hut

**5.** woodcarver

**6.** crops

**7.** costumes

**8.** values

**10.** cold

**11.** hop

**12.** sad

**13.** bear

**14.** state

## Page 72

**1.** B

**2.** D

**3.** D

**4.** C

**5.** A

**6.** C

**7.** D

**8.** B

## Page 73

Drawings will vary but should demonstrate an understanding of the underlined words.

## Page 74

Answers may vary. Possible answers are given.

**1.** angry

**2.** color

**3.** fruit

**4.** slow

**5.** sour

**6.** soft

**7.** footprint

**8.** plate; bowl

**9.** hard

## Page 75

**1.** fabulously

**2.** splendidly

**3.** marvelously

**4.** superbly

**5.** gladly

**6.** sadly

**7.** quickly

**8.** softly

Drawings will vary but should demonstrate an understanding of the new words.

## Page 76

Drawings will vary but should demonstrate an understanding of the words.

## Page 77

Answers will vary based on students' personal experiences.

## Page 79

**1.** lift

**2.** years

**3.** weight

**4.** queen

**5.** thousands

6. colony

7. hundreds

8. single

**Page 80**

1. hundreds; thousands

2. years

3. queen

4. colony

Additional words will vary.

**Page 81**
**Across**

2. weight

4. hundreds

6. queen

7. single

8. years

**Down**

1. lift

3. thousands

5. colony

**Page 82**

1. A

2. C

3. A

4. D

5. B

6. C

7. A

8. C

**Page 83**

Tiger

Drawing and label will vary but should demonstrate an understanding of the vocabulary words.

**Page 84**

Sentences and drawings will vary but should demonstrate an understanding of the vocabulary words.

**Page 85**

1. day

2. queen

3. teeth

4. see

5. bedroom

6. feet

7. St.

8. smooth

9. feathers

10. hand

**Page 86**

Drawings will vary but should demonstrate an understanding of the underlined words.

**Page 87**

Answers will vary based on students' personal experiences.



Vocabulary in Context G2, SV 9780547625751

**Page 89**

1. flock

2. chores

3. pasture

4. farmer

5. herd

6. raise

7. grazing

8. market

**Page 90**

1. b

2. a

3. a

4. b

5. a

6. b

7. b

8. a

**Page 91**

How They Eat: grazing

Where They Go: pasture

Work Done for Them: chores, raise

Groups of Them: flock, herd

Additional words will vary.

**Page 92**

1. A

2. B

3. D

4. C

5. B

6. B

7. C

8. A

**Page 93**

Drawings will vary but should demonstrate an understanding of the underlined words.

**Page 94**

Drawings or words will vary but should demonstrate an understanding of the words in the boxes.

**Page 95**

Drawings will vary but should demonstrate an understanding of the words students circle.

**Page 96**

Drawings and labels will vary.

**Page 97**

Answers will vary based on students' personal experiences.

**Page 99**

1. newspaper

2. crowded

3. repair

4. laws




**Answer Key**
Vocabulary in Context G2, SV 9780547625751

5. reporter

6. safe

7. fair

8. article

**Page 100**

1. reporter

2. newspaper

3. crowded

4. safe

5. repair

6. fair

7. article

8. laws

**Page 101**

1. repair

2. newspaper

3. crowded

4. safe

5. reporter

6. article

7. fair

8. laws

**Page 102**

1. C

2. D

3. A

4. D

5. B

6. B

7. A

8. C

**Page 103**

Drawings will vary but should demonstrate an understanding of the underlined words.

**Page 104**

1. reuse

2. rewrite

3. repaint

4. reheat

5. return

6. reunite

7. reread

8. replay

Drawings will vary but should demonstrate an understanding of the new words.

**Page 105**

Drawings will vary but should demonstrate an understanding of the categories.

**Page 106**

1. recycle

2. retrace

3. review

4. recount

5. rethink

Drawings will vary but should demonstrate an understanding of the vocabulary words.

**Page 107**
Answers will vary based on students' personal experiences.



Vocabulary in Context G2, SV 9780547625751

# My Own Word List